life. For God did not send His Son into th
rld through Him might be saved. For Go
gotten Son, that whoever believes in Hi
or God did not send His Son int the wor
ugh Him might h o love
, that whoever b uld n

D1039430

ot send His Son i ld to condem
ight be saved. For God so loved the wor
hoever believes in Him should not peri
nd His Son into the world to condemn t
be saved. For God so loved the world th
believes in Him should not perish but ha
into the world to condemn the world, b
or God so loved the world that He gave H
Him should not perish but have everlas
world to condemn the world, but that t
so loved the world that He gave His o
hould not perish but have everlasting li
to condemn the world; but that the wor
t send His Son into the world to conder
ght be saved. For God did not send His

Him should not perish but have everlas
orld to condemn the world, but that the
loved the world that He gave His only
nould not perish but have everlasting life
condemn the world, but that the world t
e world that He gave His only begotten
erish but have everlasting life. For God d
e world, but that the world through Him
at He gave His only begotten Son, that
t have everlasting life. For God did not
orld, but that the world through Him mi
e gave His only begotten Son, that whoev
erlasting life. For God did not send His
at the world through Him might be save
ly begotten Son, that whoever believes
g life. For God did not send His Son into
orld through Him might be saved. For G
gotten Son, that whoever believes in Hi
r God did not send His Son into the wo
rough Him might be saved. For God did
e world, but that the world through Him

A GIFT FOR

FROM

DATE

GOD'S PROMISES®
for NEW
BELIEVERS

BY JACK COUNTRYMAN

A Division of Thomas Nelson Publishers

THOMAS NELSON
Since 1798

NASHVILLE   MEXICO CITY   RIO DE JANEIRO

Published in Nashville, Tennessee, by Thomas Nelson. Thomas Nelson is a registered trademark of HarperCollins Christian Publishing, Inc.

Cover design by LeftCoast Design.

Thomas Nelson titles may be purchased in bulk for educational, business, fund-raising, or sales promotional use. For information, please e-mail SpecialMarkets@ ThomasNelson.com.

ISBN-13: 978-0-529-10229-4 (Hardcover)
ISBN-13: 978-0-7180-3227-2 (Softcover)

Printed in China

14 15 16 17 18 TIMS 5 4 3 2 1

www.thomasnelson.com

CONTENTS

GOD PROMISES TO BLESS BELIEVERS WHO . . .

GOD PROMISES TO GIVE HIS CHILDREN HIS . . .

GOD PROMISES TO . . .

GOD'S UNCONDITIONAL LOVE IS WITH YOU WHEN YOU . . .

INTRODUCTION

As a new or growing believer who is walking through life with Jesus as your Savior and Lord, you will find that God's promises offer you guidance, hope, and peace. His Word—the Bible—contains all that new believers, longtime believers, and believers in between need in order to grow in their relationship with Christ and to live each day mindful of His presence with them. As you read about the topics and then see what the Bible says about each, take time to think about what the verses mean and what they mean for your life. Let the Word of God be a source of knowledge, strength, and encouragement as you face life's challenges and joys.

THE BIBLE IS YOUR . . .

THE BIBLE IS YOUR . . .

DEED OF INHERITANCE

When you accepted Jesus Christ as your Savior—as the One who died on the cross, taking on the punishment you deserve for your sin—you became a Christian and a member of God's family. He has adopted you as His child and promised you, His child, eternal life in heaven.

The Spirit Himself bears witness with our spirit that we are children of God, and if children, then heirs—heirs of God and joint heirs with Christ, if indeed we suffer with Him, that we may also be glorified together.

ROMANS 8:16–17

"So now, brethren, I commend you to God and to the word of His grace, which is able to build you up and give you an inheritance among all those who are sanctified."

ACTS 20:32

In Him also we have obtained an inheritance, being predestined according to the purpose of Him who works all things according to the counsel of His will, that we who first trusted in Christ should be to the praise of His glory.

In Him you also trusted, after you heard the word of truth, the gospel of your salvation; in whom also, having believed, you were sealed with the Holy Spirit of promise, who is the guarantee of our inheritance until the redemption of the purchased possession, to the praise of His glory.

EPHESIANS 1:11–14

Blessed be the God and Father of our Lord Jesus Christ, who according to His abundant mercy has begotten us again to a living hope through the resurrection of Jesus Christ from the dead, to an inheritance incorruptible and undefiled and that does not fade away, reserved in heaven for you.

1 PETER 1:3–4

THE BIBLE IS YOUR . . .

GUIDE FOR LIFE

God cares about you so much that He has given you a guide for life. That guide is the Bible, and all of us Christians are to be students of that Book throughout our lives. We grow in our faith, we share our beliefs more clearly, and we gain a big-picture perspective on the course of history when we regularly spend time learning what God wants us to know about His love and how He wants us to respond to it. God desires for you—for all of His children—to know all you can about Him and all you can about how to live in a way that honors Him. This knowledge and wisdom are available to you in the Bible.

Your word is a lamp to my feet
And a light to my path.

PSALM 119:105

"If you abide in My word, you are My disciples
indeed. And you shall know the truth, and the truth
shall make you free."

JOHN 8:31–32

I will instruct you and teach you in the way you
should go;
I will guide you with My eye.

PSALM 32:8

"This Book of the Law shall not depart from your
mouth, but you shall meditate in it day and night, that
you may observe to do according to all that is written
in it. For then you will make your way prosperous,
and then you will have good success."

JOSHUA 1:8

How can a young man cleanse his way?
By taking heed according to Your word.

PSALM 119:9

THE BIBLE IS YOUR . . .

STABLE FOUNDATION FOR LIFE

The truths we find in the Bible nourish our faith and grow our knowledge of God and of what it means to be His child. God's Word provides a stable foundation for the lifestyle He has designed for your good and His glory. No wonder God urges you and me to pay attention to what He teaches us in His Word, to remember what those instructions are, and to follow them however countercultural they are. With its mantra of "tolerance" and its fluid morals, the world's paths are lined with snares and pitfalls. Since God's Word can help you avoid those dangers, spend time reading the Bible. Nowhere else will you find as solid a foundation for your life as God's never-changing truth.

My son, give attention to my words;
   Incline your ear to my sayings.
   Do not let them depart from your eyes;
   Keep them in the midst of your heart;
   For they are life to those who find them,
   And health to all their flesh.

PROVERBS 4:20–22

"The grass withers, the flower fades,
   But the word of our God stands forever."

ISAIAH 40:8

What then shall we say to these things? If God is for us, who can be against us?

ROMANS 8:31

"All flesh is as grass,
   And all the glory of man as the flower of the
      grass.
   The grass withers,
   And its flower falls away,
   But the word of the LORD endures forever."

1 PETER 1:24–25

"Heaven and earth will pass away, but My words will by no means pass away."

MATTHEW 24:35

SOURCE OF STRENGTH

More important than physical strength is the mental, emotional, moral, and spiritual strength we need to stay faithful to God day in and day out. No matter the circumstances, the Bible can give you fortitude—when life is hard or easy, when we feel all alone or completely loved, and when we're wandering aimlessly or serving God and feeling more fulfilled than we ever thought possible. This kind of strength comes from the Holy Spirit who is with you always and from the love God has promised every follower of Jesus Christ. The more you learn about the Bible and your faith, the stronger you will be in this world that is not always gracious to Christians. The Lord has promised to be your Rock, your Fortress, and your Deliverer, and He calls upon you to trust Him for every kind of strength you need, whatever circumstances you face. The Lord has promised to uphold you with His righteous right hand. Trust Him to do exactly that and call on Him for strength—for whatever kind of strength you need.

[I pray that God] would grant you, according to the riches of His glory, to be strengthened with might through His Spirit in the inner man, that Christ may dwell in your hearts through faith.

EPHESIANS 3:16–17

[We pray] that you may walk worthy of the Lord, fully pleasing Him, being fruitful in every good work and increasing in the knowledge of God; strengthened with all might, according to His glorious power, for all patience and longsuffering with joy; giving thanks to the Father who has qualified us to be partakers of the inheritance of the saints in the light.

COLOSSIANS 1:10–12

But those who wait on the LORD
    Shall renew their strength;
    They shall mount up with wings like eagles,
    They shall run and not be weary,
    They shall walk and not faint.

ISAIAH 40:31

"Fear not, for I am with you;
  Be not dismayed, for I am your God.
  I will strengthen you,
  Yes, I will help you,
  I will uphold you with My righteous right hand."

ISAIAH 41:10

The LORD is my rock and my fortress and my
      deliverer;
  My God, my strength, in whom I will trust;
  My shield and the horn of my salvation, my
      stronghold.

PSALM 18:2

THE BIBLE IS YOUR . . .

ABSOLUTE AUTHORITY
FOR ALL OF LIFE

Simply put, if it's in the Bible, you can believe it's true. The words in Scripture are indeed the absolute authority for every Christian and a road map for living a life that honors and glorifies Jesus. God's Word gives you the instructions you need to live each day aware of God's presence and for His glory. Never forget that God has instituted every single guideline and command for your own good!

Forever, O LORD,
    Your word is settled in heaven.

PSALM 119:89

All Scripture is given by inspiration of God, and is profitable for doctrine, for reproof, for correction, for instruction in righteousness.

2 TIMOTHY 3:16

The word of God is living and powerful, and sharper than any two-edged sword, piercing even to the division of soul and spirit, and of joints and marrow, and is a discerner of the thoughts and intents of the heart.

HEBREWS 4:12

"For as the rain comes down, and the snow
      from heaven,
  And do not return there,
  But water the earth,
  And make it bring forth and bud,
  That it may give seed to the sower
  And bread to the eater,
  So shall My word be that goes forth from
      My mouth;
  It shall not return to Me void,
  But it shall accomplish what I please,
  And it shall prosper in the thing for which I
      sent it."

ISAIAH 55:10–11

GOD
PROMISES
EVERY
BELIEVER . . .

GOD PROMISES EVERY BELIEVER . . .

HIS FAITHFULNESS

For nearly one hundred years, God's people have sung "Great Is Thy Faithfulness," proclaiming God's goodness and, yes, His faithfulness. Your Maker and the Creator of heaven and earth has been and always will be faithful to those who love Him and who have named Jesus as their Savior and Lord. In any and every situation you face, you can be sure that the Lord is with you and is working in those circumstances for your good. He will always be with you, and He will never fail you. You can know His strength and the peace of His presence every minute of every day.

"Because the Lord loves you, and because He would keep the oath which He swore to your fathers, the Lord has brought you out with a mighty hand, and redeemed you from the house of bondage, from the hand of Pharaoh king of Egypt.

Therefore know that the Lord your God, He is God, the faithful God who keeps covenant and mercy for a thousand generations with those who love Him and keep His commandments."

DEUTERONOMY 7:8–9

I will sing of the mercies of the Lord forever;
   With my mouth will I make known Your
        faithfulness to all generations.
   For I have said, "Mercy shall be built up forever;
   Your faithfulness You shall establish in the very
        heavens." . . .
"My lovingkindness I will not utterly take from him,
   Nor allow My faithfulness to fail.
   My covenant I will not break,
   Nor alter the word that has gone out of My lips."

PSALM 89:1–2, 33–34

God is faithful, by whom you were called into the fellowship of His Son, Jesus Christ our Lord.

1 CORINTHIANS 1:9

THE RETURN OF CHRIST

Have you heard the greatest promise in the Bible? Jesus Christ is coming back to earth to take His children to be with Him in heaven. No one knows the time, and no one understands all the specifics or how-tos of that promise, but every believer can trust that promise. Believers understand that their eternity in heaven is the promised victory over death achieved when Jesus died on the cross—and death is not just a heart that doesn't beat; death is separation from God. So whatever you go through in life, you can look forward to spending eternity with Jesus. That's a blessed consequence of His death on the cross.

For if we believe that Jesus died and rose again, even so God will bring with Him those who sleep in Jesus. . . . For the Lord Himself will descend from heaven with a shout, with the voice of an archangel, and with the trumpet of God. And the dead in Christ will rise first. Then we who are alive and remain shall be caught up together with them in the clouds to meet the Lord in the air. And thus we shall always be with the Lord. Therefore comfort one another with these words.

1 THESSALONIANS 4:14, 16–18

We shall not all sleep, but we shall all be changed—in a moment, in the twinkling of an eye, at the last trumpet. For the trumpet will sound, and the dead will be raised incorruptible, and we shall be changed. For this corruptible must put on incorruption, and this mortal must put on immortality. So when this corruptible has put on incorruption, and this mortal has put on immortality, then shall be brought to pass the saying that is written: "Death is swallowed up in victory."

"O Death, where is your sting?

O Hades, where is your victory?"

The sting of death is sin, and the strength of sin is

the law. But thanks be to God, who gives us the victory through our Lord Jesus Christ.

1 CORINTHIANS 15:51–57

The day of the Lord will come as a thief in the night, in which the heavens will pass away with a great noise, and the elements will melt with fervent heat; both the earth and the works that are in it will be burned up. Therefore, since all these things will be dissolved, what manner of persons ought you to be in holy conduct and godliness, looking for and hastening the coming of the day of God, because of which the heavens will be dissolved, being on fire, and the elements will melt with fervent heat? Nevertheless we, according to His promise, look for new heavens and a new earth in which righteousness dwells.

2 PETER 3:10–13

ETERNITY WITH HIM

Jesus died on the cross as the perfect, sinless sacrifice for our sin, and that's why we can know God's forgiveness and experience fellowship with Him, the Holy One. That fellowship will continue in heaven for eternity. The spirit of every human being will live forever, but only believers will have everlasting life with Jesus. You can look forward to spending eternity with Him. Nothing can change that outcome for you. You can be absolutely sure that you will live forever with Christ, free of death, sorrow, and pain and knowing the love, joy, and peace that only He can give.

This is the testimony: that God has given us eternal life, and this life is in His Son.

1 JOHN 5:11

"He who hears My word and believes in Him who sent Me has everlasting life, and shall not come into judgment, but has passed from death into life."

JOHN 5:24

We know that the Son of God has come and has given us an understanding, that we may know Him who is true; and we are in Him who is true, in His Son Jesus Christ. This is the true God and eternal life.

1 JOHN 5:20

"I am the living bread which came down from heaven. If anyone eats of this bread, he will live forever; and the bread that I shall give is My flesh, which I shall give for the life of the world."

JOHN 6:51

"I am the resurrection and the life. He who believes in Me, though he may die, he shall live. And whoever lives and believes in Me shall never die. Do you believe this?"

JOHN 11:25–26

GOD PROMISES EVERY BELIEVER . . .

WISDOM

First, a definition of wisdom. *Wisdom* is knowledge we learn by living life. It is also knowing how to apply to life what we learn. Wisdom is understanding what isn't obvious on the surface. It's being able to anticipate possible consequences. It's learning from others who have gone before or who know more than we know. God's Word is a treasure chest of this last kind of wisdom. In addition to providing us with this written source of wisdom, God will respond when we ask for wisdom for specific situations. He has promised!

If any of you lacks wisdom, let him ask of God, who gives to all liberally and without reproach, and it will be given to him.

JAMES 1:5

I will instruct you and teach you in the way you
		should go;
	I will guide you with My eye.

PSALM 32:8

This Book of the Law shall not depart from your mouth, but you shall meditate in it day and night, that you may observe to do according to all that is written in it. For then you will make your way prosperous, and then you will have good success.

JOSHUA 1:8

"When He, the Spirit of truth, has come, He will guide you into all truth; for He will not speak on His own authority, but whatever He hears He will speak; and He will tell you things to come."

JOHN 16:13

Commit your works to the LORD,
	And your thoughts will be established.

PROVERBS 16:3

ANSWERED PRAYER

Prayer is key to your relationship with God. Your talking to Him about concerns and hurts, about challenges and opportunities, plus your listening for His guidance, wisdom, and reassurance function as the lifeblood of that relationship. God calls you to "pray without ceasing" (1 Thessalonians 5:17)—and know that He who never sleeps will always hear you. Day and night God listens for the prayers of His people, and He promises to answer. Be encouraged that God will answer your prayers, regardless of whether the response is a yes, no, or wait, or perhaps a radical change of circumstances, or a comforting sense of His presence.

"Ask, and it will be given to you; seek, and you will find; knock, and it will be opened to you. For everyone who asks receives, and he who seeks finds, and to him who knocks it will be opened."

MATTHEW 7:7–8

"If you have faith and do not doubt, you will not only do what was done to the fig tree, but also if you say to this mountain, 'Be removed and be cast into the sea,' it will be done. And whatever things you ask in prayer, believing, you will receive."

MATTHEW 21:21–22

"Have faith in God. For assuredly, I say to you, whoever says to this mountain, 'Be removed and be cast into the sea,' and does not doubt in his heart, but believes that those things he says will be done, he will have whatever he says. Therefore I say to you, whatever things you ask when you pray, believe that you receive them, and you will have them."

MARK 11:22–24

"You now have sorrow; but I will see you again and your heart will rejoice, and your joy no one will take from you. . . . Most assuredly, I say to you, whatever you ask the Father in My name He will give you. . . . Ask, and you will receive, that your joy may be full."

JOHN 16:22–24

"Call to Me, and I will answer you, and show you great and mighty things, which you do not know."

JEREMIAH 33:3

JOY

Happiness and joy are not one and the same. Happiness is based on life's circumstances; joy is not. The root of *happiness—hap—*is a Middle English word that means "chance." We can feel *hap*py when life *hap*pens to be going well. We believers can know joy, though, in the midst of suffering. That's because joy takes in the big-picture perspective, embracing Jesus' death on the cross, the forgiveness of our sin, and the promise of eternal life with the Almighty and Holy God in heaven, a place without pain or tears, without sadness or suffering. This reality is always cause for rejoicing!

"These things I have spoken to you, that My joy may remain in you, and that your joy may be full. This is My commandment, that you love one another as I have loved you."

JOHN 15:11–12

But let all those rejoice who put their trust in You;
    Let them ever shout for joy, because You
        defend them;
    Let those also who love Your name
    Be joyful in You.
    For You, O LORD, will bless the righteous;
    With favor You will surround him as with a shield.

PSALM 5:11–12

"Come to Me, all you who labor and are heavy laden, and I will give you rest. Take My yoke upon you and learn from Me, for I am gentle and lowly in heart, and you will find rest for your souls. For My yoke is easy and My burden is light."

MATTHEW 11:28–30

The kingdom of God is not eating and drinking, but righteousness and peace and joy in the Holy Spirit. For he who serves Christ in these things is acceptable to God and approved by men.

ROMANS 14:17–18

Restore to me the joy of Your salvation,
   And uphold me by Your generous Spirit.
   Then I will teach transgressors Your ways,
   And sinners shall be converted to You.

PSALM 51:12–13

HOPE

Human beings have hopes and dreams. We long for certain things to happen; we hope for specific circumstances to fall into place. As people who have placed our faith in Jesus Christ, however, our hope takes on the dimension of confidence. To be specific, we can be absolutely confident that because of Jesus' death on the cross and His resurrection from the dead, we will live forever with Him, forgiven of all our sins, cleansed from sin's stains, and joyful for His graciously including us in His heavenly family.

Through the LORD's mercies we are not consumed,
    Because His compassions fail not.
    They are new every morning;
    Great is Your faithfulness.
    "The LORD is my portion," says my soul,
    "Therefore I hope in Him!"

LAMENTATIONS 3:22–24

Having been justified by faith, we have peace with God through our Lord Jesus Christ, through whom also we have access by faith into this grace in which we stand, and rejoice in hope of the glory of God. And not only that, but we also glory in tribulations, knowing that tribulation produces perseverance; and perseverance, character; and character, hope. Now hope does not disappoint, because the love of God has been poured out in our hearts by the Holy Spirit who was given to us.

ROMANS 5:1–5

Let us who are of the day be sober, putting on the breastplate of faith and love, and as a helmet the hope of salvation. For God did not appoint us to wrath, but to obtain salvation through our Lord Jesus Christ.

1 THESSALONIANS 5:8–9

HIS DIVINE PROTECTION

God is on your side! That may sound overly simplistic, but we need to cling to that basic truth when the world undermines and even attacks our faith in Jesus. God promises to guard our hearts and our minds in that battle. We also need to remember that God is on our side when we consider the absolute fact that Satan is a stronger, more deadly enemy than any of the world's threats or weapons. Eternity is at stake in the battle that matters most—the battle between holiness and evil—and God promises to protect His people.

He who dwells in the secret place of the Most High
    Shall abide under the shadow of the Almighty.
    I will say of the LORD, "He is my refuge and
        my fortress;
    My God, in Him I will trust."
Surely He shall deliver you from the snare of
        the fowler
    And from the perilous pestilence.
    He shall cover you with His feathers,
    And under His wings you shall take refuge;
    His truth shall be your shield and buckler.
    You shall not be afraid of the terror by night,
    Nor of the arrow that flies by day,
    Nor of the pestilence that walks in darkness,
    Nor of the destruction that lays waste at noonday.

                                    PSALM 91:1–6

The LORD is my light and my salvation;
    Whom shall I fear?
    The LORD is the strength of my life;
    Of whom shall I be afraid?

                                    PSALM 27:1

Be anxious for nothing, but in everything by prayer and supplication, with thanksgiving, let your requests be made known to God; and the peace of God, which surpasses all understanding, will guard your hearts and minds through Christ Jesus.

PHILIPPIANS 4:6–7

"Are not two sparrows sold for a copper coin? And not one of them falls to the ground apart from your Father's will. But the very hairs of your head are all numbered. Do not fear therefore; you are of more value than many sparrows."

MATTHEW 10:29–31

The fear of man brings a snare,
But whoever trusts in the LORD shall be safe.

PROVERBS 29:25

I will both lie down in peace, and sleep;
For You alone, O LORD, make me dwell in safety.

PSALM 4:8

HIS CONSTANT COMFORT

God is in the business of comforting His people in their sadness, loneliness, persecution, loss, and pain. In fact, you may find it easier to sense His presence with you when life is hard. The Lord has promised to always be with each of His people: He will never leave you nor forsake you. Instead, He will comfort you and strengthen you so that you can do what He calls you to do. And one thing He does want you to do is to comfort people who are hurting with the comfort that He has given you and continues to give you.

Blessed be the God and Father of our Lord Jesus Christ, the Father of mercies and God of all comfort, who comforts us in all our tribulation, that we may be able to comfort those who are in any trouble, with the comfort with which we ourselves are comforted by God.

2 CORINTHIANS 1:3–4

Sing, O heavens!
    Be joyful, O earth!
    And break out in singing, O mountains!
    For the LORD has comforted His people,
    And will have mercy on His afflicted.

ISAIAH 49:13

"Fear not, for I am with you;
    Be not dismayed, for I am your God.
    I will strengthen you,
    Yes, I will help you,
    I will uphold you with My righteous right hand."

ISAIAH 41:10

Yea, though I walk through the valley of the shadow
of death,
I will fear no evil;
For You are with me;
Your rod and Your staff, they comfort me.
You prepare a table before me in the presence of
my enemies;
You anoint my head with oil;
My cup runs over.
Surely goodness and mercy shall follow me
All the days of my life;
And I will dwell in the house of the LORD
Forever.

PSALM 23:4–6

Let, I pray, Your merciful kindness be for my comfort,
According to Your word to Your servant.
Let Your tender mercies come to me, that I
may live;
For Your law is my delight.

PSALM 119:76–77

HIS CONTINUAL ASSURANCE

God created human beings in order to be in relationship with us. The sweet fellowship He initially enjoyed with man and woman was no longer possible once humans disobeyed and sinned. Our holy God gave His Son, Jesus, to die on the cross so that He could once again be in relationship with us. Having adopted as His children those of us who have confessed our sins and chosen to live with Jesus as our Lord, God will faithfully bless us for our good and for His glory.

"Do not seek what you should eat or what you should drink, nor have an anxious mind. For all these things the nations of the world seek after, and your Father knows that you need these things. But seek the kingdom of God, and all these things shall be added to you."

LUKE 12:29–31

[Abraham] did not waver at the promise of God through unbelief, but was strengthened in faith, giving glory to God, and being fully convinced that what He had promised He was also able to perform.

ROMANS 4:20–21

The Lord is not slack concerning His promise, as some count slackness, but is longsuffering toward us, not willing that any should perish but that all should come to repentance.

2 PETER 3:9

Let us draw near with a true heart in full assurance of faith, having our hearts sprinkled from an evil conscience and our bodies washed with pure water. Let us hold fast the confession of our hope without wavering, for He who promised is faithful.

HEBREWS 10:22–23

TO BE WORTHY OF OUR CONFIDENCE

If you have named Jesus as your Savior, think about what you have been saved from and what you have been saved for. You have been saved *from* eternal separation from God and for eternity with your heavenly Father. You have been saved from a purposeless existence and in order to serve God and enjoy Him forever. Ask God for specific direction as to where He would have you serve Him and serve His people. You will know as one of His blessings a growing confidence in Him, which will mean a growing confidence for living life.

I can do all things through Christ who strengthens me.
PHILIPPIANS 4:13

Do not cast away your confidence, which has great reward. For you have need of endurance, so that after you have done the will of God, you may receive the promise.

HEBREWS 10:35–36

[I, Paul, am] confident of this very thing, that He who has begun a good work in you will complete it until the day of Jesus Christ.

PHILIPPIANS 1:6

Now this is the confidence that we have in [Jesus], that if we ask anything according to His will, He hears us. And if we know that He hears us, whatever we ask, we know that we have the petitions that we have asked of Him.

1 JOHN 5:14–15

"Most assuredly, I say to you, he who believes in Me, the works that I do he will do also; and greater works than these he will do, because I go to My Father."

JOHN 14:12

The LORD will be your confidence,
    And will keep your foot from being caught.

PROVERBS 3:26

GOD PROMISES EVERY BELIEVER . . .

JESUS AS YOUR COMPANION

The classic hymn celebrates the truth: "what a friend we have in Jesus"! When this Friend sent His Spirit to be with us—to, in fact, dwell within us—Jesus made good on His promise to be with us always. Once we name Jesus as our Savior and Lord, we are never alone: we are blessed by His companionship. He will enable us to glorify God in all that we do.

Let your conduct be without covetousness; be content with such things as you have. For He Himself has said, "I will never leave you nor forsake you."

HEBREWS 13:5

"No longer do I call you servants, for a servant does not know what his master is doing; but I have called you friends, for all things that I heard from My Father I have made known to you. You did not choose Me, but I chose you and appointed you that you should go and bear fruit, and that your fruit should remain, that whatever you ask the Father in My name He may give you."

JOHN 15:15–16

Draw near to God and He will draw near to you. Cleanse your hands, you sinners; and purify your hearts, you double-minded. . . . Humble yourselves in the sight of the Lord, and He will lift you up.

JAMES 4:8, 10

A man who has friends must himself be friendly,
   But there is a friend who sticks closer than
      a brother.

PROVERBS 18:24

I am a companion of all who fear You,
   And of those who keep Your precepts.
   The earth, O Lord, is full of Your mercy;
   Teach me Your statutes.

PSALM 119:63–64

JESUS AS YOUR SAVIOR

Jesus, the Son of God, left His Father's side in heaven, became flesh, and dwelled in this dark world for one specific purpose: taking our punishment on Himself, Jesus died on the cross so that we could be forgiven. His ultimate sacrifice saved us sinners from eternal separation from our holy God. What a wonderful Savior is Jesus your Lord!

Not by works of righteousness which we have done, but according to [God's] mercy He saved us, through the washing of regeneration and renewing of the Holy Spirit, whom He poured out on us abundantly through Jesus Christ our Savior.

TITUS 3:5–6

"God so loved the world that He gave His only begotten Son, that whoever believes in Him should not perish but have everlasting life. For God did not send His Son into the world to condemn the world, but that the world through Him might be saved."

JOHN 3:16–17

God, who is rich in mercy, because of His great love with which He loved us, even when we were dead in trespasses, made us alive together with Christ (by grace you have been saved). . . . For by grace you have been saved through faith, and that not of yourselves; it is the gift of God, not of works, lest anyone should boast.

EPHESIANS 2:4–5, 8–9

If anyone is in Christ, he is a new creation; old things have passed away; behold, all things have become new.

2 CORINTHIANS 5:17

JESUS AS YOUR EXAMPLE

One aspect of Jesus' earthly ministry was to model God-glorifying daily life. Jesus humbly came to serve. And Jesus served by teaching, by healing, and by dying for our sin. You can follow His example by serving people in your family, neighborhood, office, and church with the time, talents, and finances God has blessed you with.

To this you were called, because Christ also suffered for us, leaving us an example, that you should follow His steps.

1 PETER 2:21

"If I then, your Lord and Teacher, have washed your feet, you also ought to wash one another's feet. For I have given you an example, that you should do as I have done to you."

JOHN 13:14–15

Let this mind be in you which was also in Christ Jesus, who, being in the form of God, did not consider it robbery to be equal with God, but made Himself of no reputation, taking the form of a bondservant, and coming in the likeness of men. And being found in appearance as a man, He humbled Himself and became obedient to the point of death, even the death of the cross.

PHILIPPIANS 2:5–8

"Whoever desires to become great among you shall be your servant. And whoever of you desires to be first shall be slave of all. For even the Son of Man did not come to be served, but to serve, and to give His life a ransom for many."

MARK 10:43–45

JESUS AS YOUR SECURITY

To one degree or another, all of us human beings like security, and when we are parents, we do our best to provide our children with security. Only Jesus, however, offers genuine security and eternal security. Absolutely nothing can separate you, your children, and others you love from God's love. His love is no-fail security.

[Be] confident of this very thing, that He who has begun a good work in you will complete it until the day of Jesus Christ.

PHILIPPIANS 1:6

Blessed be the God and Father of our Lord Jesus Christ, who according to His abundant mercy has begotten us again to a living hope through the resurrection of Jesus Christ from the dead, to an inheritance incorruptible and undefiled and that does not fade away, reserved in heaven for you, who are kept by the power of God through faith for salvation ready to be revealed in the last time.

1 PETER 1:3–5

"My sheep hear My voice, and I know them, and they follow Me. And I give them eternal life, and they shall never perish; neither shall anyone snatch them out of My hand. My Father, who has given them to Me, is greater than all; and no one is able to snatch them out of My Father's hand."

JOHN 10:27–29

I am persuaded that neither death nor life, nor angels nor principalities nor powers, nor things present nor things to come, nor height nor depth, nor any other created thing, shall be able to separate us from the love of God which is in Christ Jesus our Lord.

ROMANS 8:38–39

Now to Him who is able to keep you from stumbling,
　　And to present you faultless
　　Before the presence of His glory with
　　　　exceeding joy,
　　To God our Savior,
　　Who alone is wise,
　　Be glory and majesty,
　　Dominion and power,
　　Both now and forever.
　　Amen.

JUDE vv. 24–25

JESUS AS YOUR SUFFICIENCY

Needs and wants are very different. Like a good earthly father, your heavenly Father has promised to meet your *needs*. When God calls you to serve in a certain way, for instance, He will equip you to do that work. When you ask for something according to His will, God will provide. Don't hesitate to ask God to fill you with His presence and bless you so you can serve for His glory.

God is able to make all grace abound toward you, that you, always having all sufficiency in all things, may have an abundance for every good work.

2 CORINTHIANS 9:8

"Whatever things you ask when you pray, believe
that you receive them, and you will have them."

MARK 11:24

"In that day you will ask Me nothing. Most assuredly,
I say to you, whatever you ask the Father in My
name He will give you. Until now you have asked
nothing in My name. Ask, and you will receive, that
your joy may be full."

JOHN 16:23–24

Bless the LORD, O my soul,
    And forget not all His benefits:
    Who forgives all your iniquities,
    Who heals all your diseases,
    Who redeems your life from destruction,
    Who crowns you with lovingkindness and
        tender mercies,
    Who satisfies your mouth with good things,
    So that your youth is renewed like the eagle's.

PSALM 103:2–5

GOD PROMISES *to* BLESS BELIEVERS WHO . . .

SEEK COMMUNITY WITH OTHER BELIEVERS

God created human beings with the need to be in community. He Himself is the Triune (meaning "three-part") God: He exists as Father, Son (Jesus Christ), and Holy Spirit—and this Trinity is beyond human explanation. God wants His children to be in fellowship with Him, but our fellowship with one another is also important. God has given each person who follows Jesus a specific gift so that we can serve one another and talk about Jesus to people who don't yet know Him. Together, God's people encourage one another, teach one another, and love one another. The world can't help but notice something special about God's people!

This is the message which we have heard from Him and declare to you, that God is light and in Him is no darkness at all. If we say that we have fellowship with Him, and walk in darkness, we lie and do not practice the truth. But if we walk in the light as He is in the light, we have fellowship with one another, and the blood of Jesus Christ His Son cleanses us from all sin.

1 JOHN 1:5–7

If there is any consolation in Christ, if any comfort of love, if any fellowship of the Spirit, if any affection and mercy, fulfill my joy by being like-minded, having the same love, being of one accord, of one mind. Let nothing be done through selfish ambition or conceit, but in lowliness of mind let each esteem others better than himself. Let each of you look out not only for his own interests, but also for the interests of others.

PHILIPPIANS 2:1–4

Let the word of Christ dwell in you richly in all wisdom, teaching and admonishing one another in psalms and hymns and spiritual songs, singing with grace in your hearts to the Lord.

COLOSSIANS 3:16

When the Day of Pentecost had fully come, they were all with one accord in one place. . . . And [the new believers] continued steadfastly in the apostles' doctrine and fellowship, in the breaking of bread, and in prayers. . . . So continuing daily with one accord in the temple, and breaking bread from house to house, they ate their food with gladness and simplicity of heart, praising God and having favor with all the people. And the Lord added to the church daily those who were being saved.

ACTS 2:1, 42, 46–47

SERVE HIM

When we try to get our mind around just how much God loves us, we can't help but want to show our love for Him by obeying Him and by serving Him and other people—and doing so with gladness. Designed for a life of service and following Jesus' example of serving God, you will know—despite the circumstances of your days—the joy and peace that come with doing what God created you to do. Serving God also brings you into a closer relationship with Jesus, who loves you with a love that will last throughout eternity.

"No one can serve two masters; for either he will hate the one and love the other, or else he will be loyal to the one and despise the other. You cannot serve God and mammon."

MATTHEW 6:24

"Take careful heed . . . to love the LORD your God, to walk in all His ways, to keep His commandments, to hold fast to Him, and to serve Him with all your heart and with all your soul."

JOSHUA 22:5

"Choose for yourselves this day whom you will serve, whether the gods which your fathers served that were on the other side of the River, or the gods of the Amorites, in whose land you dwell. But as for me and my house, we will serve the LORD."

JOSHUA 24:15

Make a joyful shout to the LORD, all you lands!
    Serve the LORD with gladness;
    Come before His presence with singing. . . .
Enter into His gates with thanksgiving,
    And into His courts with praise.
    Be thankful to Him, and bless His name.

PSALM 100:1–2, 4

OBEY HIM

God expects His people to live according to His standards, not the world's. Our obedience to the guidelines and commands He gives us in the Bible is one way we show God our love. This obedience comes more easily when we remember that Jesus took our punishment for our sins on Himself when He died on the cross. Furthermore, our heavenly Father knows what is best for us, so our obedience is for our own good even as it honors and glorifies Him.

"Obey My voice, and I will be your God, and you shall be My people. And walk in all the ways that I have commanded you, that it may be well with you."

JEREMIAH 7:23

"If you love Me, keep My commandments. . . . He who has My commandments and keeps them, it is he who loves Me. And he who loves Me will be loved by My Father, and I will love him and manifest Myself to him."

JOHN 14:15, 21

By this we know that we know Him, if we keep His commandments. He who says, "I know Him," and does not keep His commandments, is a liar, and the truth is not in him. But whoever keeps His word, truly the love of God is perfected in him. By this we know that we are in Him. He who says he abides in Him ought himself also to walk just as He walked.

1 JOHN 2:3–6

Whatever you do, do it heartily, as to the Lord and not to men, knowing that from the Lord you will receive the reward of the inheritance; for you serve the Lord Christ.

COLOSSIANS 3:23–24

WANT THEIR LIVES TO REFLECT HIS LOVE

You've probably noticed that actions can speak louder than words. So for a minute think about what your actions say about you: Do they suggest that you are living for yourself, or do people see something different about the way you speak, work, and interact with others? Do your actions and your words shine forth God's love and the joy of being in His presence however tough life's circumstances are? The way you walk and the way you talk are opportunities to let God love others through you. When they ask what makes you different, you can tell them about Jesus and His love for them.

"You are the salt of the earth; but if the salt loses its flavor, how shall it be seasoned? It is then good for nothing but to be thrown out and trampled underfoot by men.

"You are the light of the world. A city that is set on a hill cannot be hidden. Nor do they light a lamp and put it under a basket, but on a lampstand, and it gives light to all who are in the house. Let your light so shine before men, that they may see your good works and glorify your Father in heaven."

MATTHEW 5:13–16

"I was hungry and you gave Me food; I was thirsty and you gave Me drink; I was a stranger and you took Me in; I was naked and you clothed Me; I was sick and you visited Me; I was in prison and you came to Me.'

"Then the righteous will answer Him, saying, 'Lord, when did we see You hungry and feed You, or thirsty and give You drink? When did we see You a stranger and take You in, or naked and clothe You? Or when did we see You sick, or in prison, and come to You?' And the King will answer and say to them, 'Assuredly, I say to you, inasmuch as you did it to one of the least of these My brethren, you did it to Me.'"

MATTHEW 25:35–40

If a man is overtaken in any trespass, you who are spiritual restore such a one in a spirit of gentleness, considering yourself lest you also be tempted. Bear one another's burdens, and so fulfill the law of Christ. For if anyone thinks himself to be something, when he is nothing, he deceives himself.

GALATIANS 6:1–3

By this we know love, because He laid down His life for us. And we also ought to lay down our lives for the brethren. But whoever has this world's goods, and sees his brother in need, and shuts up his heart from him, how does the love of God abide in him?

My little children, let us not love in word or in tongue, but in deed and in truth.

1 JOHN 3:16–18

WANT TO GROW SPIRITUALLY

Back in the thirteenth century, the godly Richard of Chichester prayed to God that he would "see thee more clearly, love thee more dearly, and follow thee more nearly, day by day." This timeless prayer captures the essence of a Christ-centered life: we are to continually grow in knowledge, in understanding, in wisdom, and in closeness to God. So make some time every day to be alone, read the Bible, think about what you read, and pray. God will bless you in those times even as He uses them to grow your faith and prepare you for future service to His people and in the world.

As newborn babes, desire the pure milk of the word, that you may grow thereby, if indeed you have tasted that the Lord is gracious.

1 PETER 2:2–3

But also for this very reason, giving all diligence, add to your faith virtue, to virtue knowledge, to knowledge self-control, to self-control perseverance, to perseverance godliness, to godliness brotherly kindness, and to brotherly kindness love. For if these things are yours and abound, you will be neither barren nor unfruitful in the knowledge of our Lord Jesus Christ.

2 PETER 1:5–8

[We] do not cease to pray for you, and to ask that you may be filled with the knowledge of His will in all wisdom and spiritual understanding; that you may walk worthy of the Lord, fully pleasing Him, being fruitful in every good work and increasing in the knowledge of God; strengthened with all might, according to His glorious power, for all patience and longsuffering with joy.

COLOSSIANS 1:9–11

I bow my knees to the Father of our Lord Jesus Christ . . . that He would grant you, according to the riches of His glory, to be strengthened with might through His Spirit in the inner man, that Christ may dwell in your hearts through faith; that you, being rooted and grounded in love, may be able to comprehend with all the saints what is the width and length and depth and height—to know the love of Christ which passes knowledge; that you may be filled with all the fullness of God.

EPHESIANS 3:14, 16–19

WANT TO PLEASE HIM

Webster's defines *ambassador* as "an authorized representative or messenger." As a follower of Jesus, you are His ambassador in this world. You represent His love by treating people the way you would like to be treated. You also stand ready to explain the gospel message of hope to people who ask. You live with purpose: you want to honor Jesus, your Savior, in all you say and do. And you readily share your story: "There was a time when I didn't know Jesus, but now I know Him and His forgiveness for my sin, His immeasurable love, His purpose for my life, and the promise of life eternal with Him in heaven."

"God is Spirit, and those who worship Him must worship in spirit and truth."

JOHN 4:24

You are a chosen generation, a royal priesthood, a holy nation, His own special people, that you may proclaim the praises of Him who called you out of darkness into His marvelous light.

1 PETER 2:9

Let us continually offer the sacrifice of praise to God, that is, the fruit of our lips, giving thanks to His name. But do not forget to do good and to share, for with such sacrifices God is well pleased.

HEBREWS 13:15–16

[We] do not cease to pray for you . . . that you may walk worthy of the Lord, fully pleasing Him, being fruitful in every good work and increasing in the knowledge of God; strengthened with all might, according to His glorious power, for all patience and longsuffering with joy; giving thanks to the Father who has qualified us to be partakers of the inheritance of the saints in the light.

COLOSSIANS 1:9–12

FORGIVE OTHERS

Like all of God's commands, His command to forgive those who have wronged us is for our own good. As Lewis Smedes put it, "To forgive is to set a prisoner free and discover that the prisoner was you." Besides making us a prisoner to a memory or to our anger, our lack of forgiveness can weaken our relationship with God and interfere with, if not derail, our relationship with others. Furthermore, the sins Christ has forgiven you for cost Him His life. So forgive those people you need to forgive. Find freedom for yourself—and perhaps get them curious about Jesus!

"If your brother sins against you, rebuke him; and if he repents, forgive him."

LUKE 17:3

"If you forgive men their trespasses, your heavenly Father will also forgive you. But if you do not forgive men their trespasses, neither will your Father forgive your trespasses."

MATTHEW 6:14–15

Then Peter came to [Jesus] and said, "Lord, how often shall my brother sin against me, and I forgive him? Up to seven times?"

Jesus said to him, "I do not say to you, up to seven times, but up to seventy times seven."

MATTHEW 18:21–22

"Whenever you stand praying, if you have anything against anyone, forgive him, that your Father in heaven may also forgive you your trespasses."

MARK 11:25

Put on tender mercies, kindness, humility, meekness, longsuffering; bearing with one another, and forgiving one another, if anyone has a complaint against another; even as Christ forgave you, so you also must do.

COLOSSIANS 3:12–13

REJOICE IN THE LIBERTY IN CHRIST

In the Old Testament, the people of God knew what to do about their sin: they sacrificed a perfect lamb, they accepted that their sins were forgiven, and they would start afresh to try to keep God's law. In the New Testament, the people of God still sinned, but then the perfect Lamb was sacrificed. Two thousand years ago, once and for all, the sins of God's people were forgiven. We still try to keep God's law—His perfect law of love for Him and for others—but we are free from the consequences of not measuring up to God's law. *That* is liberty in Christ—a gift we don't deserve. But that's what grace is: unmerited favor. Amazing grace!

There is therefore now no condemnation to those who are in Christ Jesus, who do not walk according to the flesh, but according to the Spirit. For the law of the Spirit of life in Christ Jesus has made me free from the law of sin and death.

ROMANS 8:1–2

You, brethren, have been called to liberty; only do not use liberty as an opportunity for the flesh, but through love serve one another.

GALATIANS 5:13

He who looks into the perfect law of liberty and continues in it, and is not a forgetful hearer but a doer of the work, this one will be blessed in what he does.

JAMES 1:25

"If you abide in My word, you are My disciples indeed. And you shall know the truth, and the truth shall make you free. . . . Therefore if the Son makes you free, you shall be free indeed."

JOHN 8:31–32, 36

The Lord is the Spirit; and where the Spirit of the Lord is, there is liberty. But we all, with unveiled face, beholding as in a mirror the glory of the Lord, are being transformed into the same image from glory to glory, just as by the Spirit of the Lord.

2 CORINTHIANS 3:17–18

This is the will of God, that by doing good you may put to silence the ignorance of foolish men—as free, yet not using liberty as a cloak for vice, but as bondservants of God. Honor all people. Love the brotherhood. Fear God. Honor the king.

1 PETER 2:15–17

SEEK WAYS TO GIVE TO GOD'S WORK

God doesn't need our money. He can run the world—He can run all of creation—without our financial aid. But God wants us to trust Him, and our giving to Him of our time, talents, and treasures shows that we trust Him. When we cling to God, when we trust in Him to be our ultimate Provider, we don't need to cling to our money. Giving to support God's work is one way we worship our good and generous heavenly Father. May we do so regularly as part of our lifestyle as God's people—and may we do so cheerfully.

"Do not lay up for yourselves treasures on earth, where moth and rust destroy and where thieves break in and steal; but lay up for yourselves treasures in heaven, where neither moth nor rust destroys and where thieves do not break in and steal. For where your treasure is, there your heart will be also."

MATTHEW 6:19–21

[Jesus] saw how the people put money into the treasury. And many who were rich put in much. Then one poor widow came and threw in two mites. . . . He called His disciples to Himself and said to them, "Assuredly, I say to you that this poor widow has put in more than all those who have given to the treasury; for they all put in out of their abundance, but she out of her poverty put in all that she had, her whole livelihood."

MARK 12:41–44

Give to the LORD the glory due His name;
    Bring an offering, and come before Him.
    Oh, worship the LORD in the beauty of holiness!

1 CHRONICLES 16:29

He who sows sparingly will also reap sparingly, and he who sows bountifully will also reap bountifully. So let each one give as he purposes in his heart, not grudgingly or of necessity; for God loves a cheerful giver.

2 CORINTHIANS 9:6–7

On the first day of the week let each one of you lay something aside.

1 CORINTHIANS 16:2

There is one who scatters, yet increases more;
  And there is one who withholds more than
      is right,
  But it leads to poverty.
  The generous soul will be made rich,
  And he who waters will also be watered himself.

PROVERBS 11:24–25

GOD PROMISES *to* GIVE HIS CHILDREN HIS . . .

LOVE

Implicit in God's great love for each of His people is the promise that He will never stop loving you, that you can do nothing to make Him love you more or less. God's love was clearly revealed in the sacrificial love that His only Son, Jesus Christ, demonstrated on the cross. Such self-sacrificial love is to characterize the love we believers have for one another. Such a lifestyle of love blesses those you come in contact with, attracts them to Jesus, and honors God.

Whoever keeps His word, truly the love of God is perfected in him. By this we know that we are in Him.

1 JOHN 2:5

Beloved, let us love one another, for love is of God; and everyone who loves is born of God and knows God. He who does not love does not know God, for God is love. In this the love of God was manifested toward us, that God has sent His only begotten Son into the world, that we might live through Him.

1 JOHN 4:7–9

Whoever believes that Jesus is the Christ is born of God, and everyone who loves Him who begot also loves him who is begotten of Him. By this we know that we love the children of God, when we love God and keep His commandments. For this is the love of God, that we keep His commandments. And His commandments are not burdensome. For whatever is born of God overcomes the world. And this is the victory that has overcome the world—our faith.

1 JOHN 5:1–4

Hope does not disappoint, because the love of God has been poured out in our hearts by the Holy Spirit who was given to us.

ROMANS 5:5

GOD PROMISES TO GIVE HIS CHILDREN HIS . . .

GRACE

Grace has been defined as "undeserved favor," and God's allowing Jesus to take the punishment and die for our sins is definitely an act of grace. Amazing grace. Yet we also experience God's grace when He blesses us in any of the countless ways He does: we haven't earned and we don't deserve family or friends, food or shelter, freedom, purpose, or hope. We experience God's grace when He provides the strength, the comfort, and His reassuring presence whenever we encounter challenges, loss, or pain. Again, amazing grace.

For the Lord God is a sun and shield;
    The Lord will give grace and glory;
    No good thing will He withhold
    From those who walk uprightly.

PSALM 84:11

Concerning this thing I pleaded with the Lord three times that it might depart from me. And He said to me, "My grace is sufficient for you, for My strength is made perfect in weakness." Therefore most gladly I will rather boast in my infirmities, that the power of Christ may rest upon me. Therefore I take pleasure in infirmities, in reproaches, in needs, in persecutions, in distresses, for Christ's sake. For when I am weak, then I am strong.

2 CORINTHIANS 12:8–10

In Him we have redemption through His blood, the forgiveness of sins, according to the riches of His grace which He made to abound toward us in all wisdom and prudence.

EPHESIANS 1:7–8

Therefore, brethren, stand fast and hold the traditions which you were taught, whether by word or our epistle.

Now may our Lord Jesus Christ Himself, and our God and Father, who has loved us and given us everlasting consolation and good hope by grace, comfort your hearts and establish you in every good word and work.

2 THESSALONIANS 2:15–17

Humble yourselves under the mighty hand of God, that He may exalt you in due time, casting all your care upon Him, for He cares for you.

Be sober, be vigilant; because your adversary the devil walks about like a roaring lion, seeking whom he may devour. Resist him, steadfast in the faith, knowing that the same sufferings are experienced by your brotherhood in the world. But may the God of all grace, who called us to His eternal glory by Christ Jesus, after you have suffered a while, perfect, establish, strengthen, and settle you.

1 PETER 5:6–10

SPIRIT

When you recognized both your sin and the fact that Jesus' death meant forgiveness for that sin, the Spirit of God started to change your heart. As He continues to work in your heart—or, in biblical terms, as He dwells in your heart, making you a temple of God Himself—you become more and more like Jesus. In addition to doing this work of transformation, the Spirit is also a teacher of God's Word, a comforter, a guide, and a prayer warrior for you.

Those who are in the flesh cannot please God.

But you are not in the flesh but in the Spirit, if indeed the Spirit of God dwells in you. Now if anyone does not have the Spirit of Christ, he is not His. And if Christ is in you, the body is dead because of sin, but the Spirit is life because of righteousness. But if the Spirit of Him who raised Jesus from the dead dwells in you, He who raised Christ from the dead will also give life to your mortal bodies through His Spirit who dwells in you.

ROMANS 8:8–11

When one turns to the Lord, the veil is taken away. Now the Lord is the Spirit; and where the Spirit of the Lord is, there is liberty. But we all, with unveiled face, beholding as in a mirror the glory of the Lord, are being transformed into the same image from glory to glory, just as by the Spirit of the Lord.

2 CORINTHIANS 3:16–18

Do you not know that you are the temple of God and that the Spirit of God dwells in you? If anyone defiles the temple of God, God will destroy him. For the temple of God is holy, which temple you are.

1 CORINTHIANS 3:16–17

"Eye has not seen, nor ear heard,
Nor have entered into the heart of man
The things which God has prepared for those
who love Him."
But God has revealed [those things] to us through
His Spirit. For the Spirit searches all things, yes,
the deep things of God. For what man knows the
things of a man except the spirit of the man which
is in him? Even so no one knows the things of God
except the Spirit of God. Now we have received, not
the spirit of the world, but the Spirit who is from God,
that we might know the things that have been freely
given to us by God.

1 CORINTHIANS 2:9–12

COMPASSION

The idea of submitting has gotten a bad rap. Depending on whom we choose to submit to, that decision can be the best we ever make. Naming Jesus as your Lord is an act of submitting to Him, but consider the nature of the God you have chosen to serve. He is compassionate and loving. He casts your confessed sins into the sea, promising not to hold them against you. He sees Jesus' sinless glory when He looks at you. He is slow to get angry with us obstinate, self-centered human beings; He is merciful and gracious to us instead. And He will be this way always—for us and for believing generations to come.

The Lᴏʀᴅ is gracious and full of compassion,
Slow to anger and great in mercy.
The Lᴏʀᴅ is good to all,
And His tender mercies are over all His works.

PSALM 145:8–9

Who is a God like You,
Pardoning iniquity
And passing over the transgression of the
remnant of His heritage?
He does not retain His anger forever,
Because He delights in mercy.
He will again have compassion on us,
And will subdue our iniquities.

MICAH 7:18–19

But You, O Lord, are a God full of compassion,
and gracious,
Longsuffering and abundant in mercy and truth.
Oh, turn to me, and have mercy on me!
Give Your strength to Your servant,
And save the son of Your maidservant.

PSALM 86:15–16

Your name, O Lord, endures forever,
Your fame, O Lord, throughout all generations.
For the Lord will judge His people,
And He will have compassion on His servants.

PSALM 135:13–14

Is there unrighteousness with God? Certainly
not! For He says to Moses, "I will have mercy
on whomever I will have mercy, and I will have
compassion on whomever I will have compassion."

ROMANS 9:14–15

All of you be of one mind, having compassion for
one another; love as brothers, be tenderhearted,
be courteous; not returning evil for evil or reviling
for reviling, but on the contrary blessing, knowing
that you were called to this, that you may inherit a
blessing.

1 PETER 3:8–9

MERCY

Grace and mercy are complimentary and invaluable blessings God pours out on us, His children. *Grace* is getting from God what we don't deserve; *mercy* is not getting from God the punishment we absolutely do deserve. Of course our best response would be heartfelt thanksgiving and gratitude.

Blessed be the God and Father of our Lord Jesus Christ, who according to His abundant mercy has begotten us again to a living hope through the resurrection of Jesus Christ from the dead.

1 PETER 1:3

Oh, give thanks to the LORD, for He is good!
  For His mercy endures forever.

1 CHRONICLES 16:34

Have mercy upon me, O God,
  According to Your lovingkindness;
  According to the multitude of Your tender
      mercies,
  Blot out my transgressions.
  Wash me thoroughly from my iniquity,
  And cleanse me from my sin.

PSALM 51:1–2

Oh, give thanks to the LORD, for He is good!
  For His mercy endures forever.
  Let the redeemed of the LORD say so,
  Whom He has redeemed from the hand of
      the enemy,
  And gathered out of the lands,
  From the east and from the west,
  From the north and from the south.

PSALM 107:1–3

FAITHFULNESS

God will be forever faithful to His character, to His children, and to His promises. God will always be loving, merciful, gracious, compassionate, wise, powerful, and sovereign. God will always protect, provide for, guide, and bless His children and their children and their children's children: He will be faithful to all generations. And God the Promise-Maker will always be the Promise-Keeper. Great is the Lord's faithfulness!

No temptation has overtaken you except such as is common to man; but God is faithful, who will not allow you to be tempted beyond what you are able, but with the temptation will also make the way of escape, that you may be able to bear it.

1 CORINTHIANS 10:13

Your mercy, O Lord, is in the heavens;
    Your faithfulness reaches to the clouds.
    Your righteousness is like the great mountains;
    Your judgments are a great deep;
    O Lord, You preserve man and beast.
How precious is Your lovingkindness, O God!
    Therefore the children of men put their trust
        under the shadow of Your wings.

PSALM 36:5–7

Let us draw near with a true heart in full assurance
of faith, having our hearts sprinkled from an evil
conscience and our bodies washed with pure water.
Let us hold fast the confession of our hope without
wavering, for He who promised is faithful. And let
us consider one another in order to stir up love and
good works.

HEBREWS 10:22–24

I will sing of the mercies of the Lord forever;
    With my mouth will I make known Your
        faithfulness to all generations.
    For I have said, "Mercy shall be built up forever;
    Your faithfulness You shall establish in the very
        heavens."

PSALM 89:1–2

KINDNESS

Just as our kindness to others shows our love for them, God's kindness to us is evidence of His great love for us. Not only does He want the very best for you, His child, but He yearns to be a part of your daily life so that, 24/7, He can shower His kindness upon you. Then, according to God's plan, we show His love and kindness to others. We let our love and kindness reflect God's love and kindness.

Let all bitterness, wrath, anger, clamor, and evil speaking be put away from you, with all malice. And be kind to one another, tenderhearted, forgiving one another, even as God in Christ forgave you.

EPHESIANS 4:31–32

Blessed be the LORD,
>For He has shown me His marvelous
>>kindness. . . !

Oh, love the LORD, all you His saints!
>For the LORD preserves the faithful,
>And fully repays the proud person.
>Be of good courage,
>And He shall strengthen your heart,
>All you who hope in the LORD.

PSALM 31:21, 23–24

Praise the LORD, all you Gentiles!
>Laud Him, all you peoples!
>For His merciful kindness is great toward us,
>and the truth of the LORD endures forever.

Praise the LORD!

PSALM 117:1–2

For the mountains shall depart
>And the hills be removed,
>But My kindness shall not depart from you,
>Nor shall My covenant of peace be removed,"
>Says the LORD, who has mercy on you.

ISAIAH 54:10

PATIENCE

Since the beginning of time God has been patient, and since He is the same yesterday, today, and tomorrow, He will be patient today and into eternity. He is patient with our pattern of sinning, asking forgiveness, doing well for a while, then sinning again, asking forgiveness, doing well for a while—you know how it goes. God is also patient when we don't love Him with all we are and when we don't love others as ourselves. When we choose to be patient with others, we give them a glimpse of God's great patience with us.

Pursue righteousness, godliness, faith, love, patience, gentleness. Fight the good fight of faith.

1 TIMOTHY 6:11–12

Whatever things were written before were written for our learning, that we through the patience and comfort of the Scriptures might have hope.

ROMANS 15:4

Count it all joy when you fall into various trials, knowing that the testing of your faith produces patience. But let patience have its perfect work, that you may be perfect and complete, lacking nothing.

JAMES 1:2–4

May the Lord direct your hearts into the love of God and into the patience of Christ.

2 THESSALONIANS 3:5

FORGIVENESS

Forgiveness is evidence of both God's mercy and His grace. He extends forgiveness rather than the punishment we deserve: that is mercy, not getting what we do deserve. And being as just as He is merciful and gracious, God allowed His Son to pay the price for our sin: that is grace, getting what we absolutely don't deserve. According to the perfect plan of our just, merciful, and gracious God, Jesus' death on the cross enables us forgiven sinners to be in relationship with our heavenly Father now and for eternity.

Bless the Lord, O my soul;
    And all that is within me, bless His holy name!
    Bless the Lord, O my soul,
    And forget not all His benefits:
    Who forgives all your iniquities,
    Who heals all your diseases,
    Who redeems your life from destruction,
    Who crowns you with lovingkindness and tender
        mercies.

PSALM 103:1–4

The Lord is merciful and gracious,
    Slow to anger, and abounding in mercy.
    He will not always strive with us,
    Nor will He keep His anger forever.
    He has not dealt with us according to our sins,
    Nor punished us according to our iniquities.
For as the heavens are high above the earth,
    So great is His mercy toward those who fear Him;
    As far as the east is from the west,
    So far has He removed our transgressions
        from us.

PSALM 103:8–12

If we say that we have no sin, we deceive ourselves, and the truth is not in us. If we confess our sins, He is faithful and just to forgive us our sins and to cleanse us from all unrighteousness.

1 JOHN 1:8–9

Lord, hear my voice!
    Let Your ears be attentive
    To the voice of my supplications.
If You, LORD, should mark iniquities,
    O Lord, who could stand?
    But there is forgiveness with You,
    That You may be feared.
I wait for the LORD, my soul waits,
    And in His word I do hope.

PSALM 130:2–5

[Give] thanks to the Father who has qualified us to be partakers of the inheritance of the saints in the light. He has delivered us from the power of darkness and conveyed us into the kingdom of the Son of His love, in whom we have redemption through His blood, the forgiveness of sins.

COLOSSIANS 1:12–14

RIGHTEOUSNESS

Jesus was the perfect Lamb of God, unblemished by sin and therefore qualified to be the once-for-all sacrifice for humanity's sins. And our sovereign and gracious God attributes Jesus' righteousness to us. There is absolutely nothing we sinners can do to cleanse ourselves of our sin or to bridge the immeasurable gap between us and our holy God. When we choose to accept His divine arrangement, though, we are blessed to have Jesus' righteousness credited to us. We are righteous not because of who we are or what we've done, but only because God chooses to accept Jesus' sacrifice and credit it to your account and mine.

If you confess with your mouth the Lord Jesus and believe in your heart that God has raised Him from the dead, you will be saved. For with the heart one believes unto righteousness, and with the mouth confession is made unto salvation.

ROMANS 10:9–10

Take up the whole armor of God, that you may be able to withstand in the evil day, and having done all, to stand.

Stand therefore, having girded your waist with truth, having put on the breastplate of righteousness, and having shod your feet with the preparation of the gospel of peace; above all, taking the shield of faith with which you will be able to quench all the fiery darts of the wicked one. And take the helmet of salvation, and the sword of the Spirit, which is the word of God.

EPHESIANS 6:13–17

He who has clean hands and a pure heart,
    Who has not lifted up his soul to an idol,
    Nor sworn deceitfully.
    He shall receive blessing from the LORD,
    And righteousness from the God of his salvation.

PSALM 24:4–5

COMFORT

Jesus walked this planet: He knows from experience the pain that comes from living in this fallen world. That knowledge enables Jesus to come alongside us—in any and all situations—with comfort for our minds and emotions, for our spirits and our souls. He is always there to remind us of His great love for us, a love evident in His broken and bleeding body on the cross. As we receive the Lord's comfort, we can also know His peace and hope when circumstances don't change.

"I will extend peace to [Jerusalem] like a river,
  And the glory of the Gentiles like a flowing stream.
  Then you shall feed;
  On her sides shall you be carried,
  And be dandled on her knees.
  As one whom his mother comforts,
  So I will comfort you;
  And you shall be comforted in Jerusalem."

ISAIAH 66:12–13

This is my comfort in my affliction,
  For Your word has given me life.
  The proud have me in great derision,
  Yet I do not turn aside from Your law.
  I remembered Your judgments of old, O LORD,
  And have comforted myself.

PSALM 119:50–52

Now may our Lord Jesus Christ Himself, and our God and Father, who has loved us and given us everlasting consolation and good hope by grace, comfort your hearts and establish you in every good word and work.

2 THESSALONIANS 2:16–17

GOD PROMISES TO GIVE HIS CHILDREN HIS . . .

POWER

An amazing truth among the amazing truths in God's Word is the fact that "the Spirit of Him who raised Jesus from the dead dwells in you" (Romans 8:11). A power stronger than death is a power not to be ignored, and that power is available to you. God's Spirit will give you strength when you are weak, overwhelmed, discouraged, exhausted—physically, mentally, emotionally, and spiritually. God's Spirit gives you the power to live each day, whatever the circumstances.

Have you not known?
Have you not heard?
The everlasting God, the Lord,
The Creator of the ends of the earth,
Neither faints nor is weary.
His understanding is unsearchable.
He gives power to the weak,
And to those who have no might He increases
strength.
Even the youths shall faint and be weary,
And the young men shall utterly fall,
But those who wait on the Lord
Shall renew their strength;
They shall mount up with wings like eagles,
They shall run and not be weary,
They shall walk and not faint.

ISAIAH 40:28–31

"Most assuredly, I say to you, he who believes in Me, the works that I do he will do also; and greater works than these he will do, because I go to My Father. And whatever you ask in My name, that I will do, that the Father may be glorified in the Son."

JOHN 14:12–13

PRESENCE

As you walk with God and keep Him the Lord and Master of your life, remember that He has promised to be with you always. Take advantage of the fact that you can have constant communication with Him as you live each day in His presence. Make it your prayer to be keenly aware of His sweet presence that guides, comforts, and strengthens. In addition to walking with Him through each day, be sure to make time to sit quietly in His presence.

Christ has not entered the holy places made with hands, which are copies of the true, but into heaven itself, now to appear in the presence of God for us.

HEBREWS 9:24

Those who trust in the LORD
    Are like Mount Zion,
    Which cannot be moved, but abides forever.
    As the mountains surround Jerusalem,
    So the LORD surrounds His people
    From this time forth and forever.

PSALM 125:1–2

"Be strong and of good courage, do not fear nor be afraid of them; for the LORD your God, He is the One who goes with you. He will not leave you nor forsake you."

DEUTERONOMY 31:6

I know that the LORD will maintain
    The cause of the afflicted,
    And justice for the poor.
    Surely the righteous shall give thanks to Your
        name;
    The upright shall dwell in Your presence.

PSALM 140:12–13

BLESSING

There is no greater blessing—for the present, for eternity—than being one of God's children. Your heavenly Father longs to bless you according to His good and perfect plans for you. He will bless you with tangibles—food, clothing, shelter, family, friends— as well as with intangibles—His mercy, grace, hope, guidance, and comfort. And, by the power of His Holy Spirit, God will fill your life with love, joy, peace, longsuffering, kindness, goodness, faithfulness, gentleness, and self-control. May your awareness of this generous outpouring of blessings enable you to walk this earth with gratitude and joy.

"Bring all the tithes into the storehouse,
    That there may be food in My house,
    And try Me now in this,"
    Says the LORD of hosts,
    "If I will not open for you the windows of heaven
    And pour out for you such blessing
    That there will not be room enough to receive it."

MALACHI 3:10

Blessed be the Lord,
    Who daily loads us with benefits,
    The God of our salvation!

PSALM 68:19

Blessed be the LORD,
    For He has shown me His marvelous kindness in
        a strong city! . . .
Oh, love the LORD, all you His saints!
    For the LORD preserves the faithful,
    And fully repays the proud person.
    Be of good courage,
    And He shall strengthen your heart,
    All you who hope in the LORD.

PSALM 31:21, 23–24

GOD PROMISES TO GIVE HIS CHILDREN HIS . . .

PEACE

O nly enmity can exist between sin and holiness, between sinful human beings and the holy Lord God. When Jesus died on the cross, He provided the way to peace: sinful human beings who acknowledge both their sin and the sacrificial death of sinless Jesus on their behalf can enter God's holy presence. In addition to this salvation peace, God gives us peace in difficult circumstances, in painful situations when peace makes little, if any, sense. That peace is one of the blessings that comes when we choose to trust Jesus with our life.

Let the peace of God rule in your hearts, to which also you were called in one body; and be thankful.

COLOSSIANS 3:15

Open the gates,
    That the righteous nation which keeps the truth
        may enter in.
    You will keep him in perfect peace,
    Whose mind is stayed on You,
    Because he trusts in You.
    Trust in the LORD forever,
    For in YAH, the LORD, is everlasting strength.

ISAIAH 26:2–4

Be anxious for nothing, but in everything by prayer and supplication, with thanksgiving, let your requests be made known to God; and the peace of God, which surpasses all understanding, will guard your hearts and minds through Christ Jesus.

PHILIPPIANS 4:6–7

"These things I have spoken to you, that in Me you may have peace. In the world you will have tribulation; but be of good cheer, I have overcome the world."

JOHN 16:33

Having been justified by faith, we have peace with God through our Lord Jesus Christ, through whom also we have access by faith into this grace in which we stand, and rejoice in hope of the glory of God.

ROMANS 5:1–2

"Peace I leave with you, My peace I give to you; not as the world gives do I give to you. Let not your heart be troubled, neither let it be afraid. You have heard Me say to you, 'I am going away and coming back to you.' If you loved Me, you would rejoice because I said, 'I am going to the Father,' for My Father is greater than I."

JOHN 14:27–28

[Jesus] is our peace, who has made both one, and has broken down the middle wall of separation, having abolished in His flesh the enmity, that is, the law of commandments contained in ordinances, so as to create in Himself one new man from the two, thus making peace.

EPHESIANS 2:14–15

GUIDANCE

God knows that the world makes many promises about what satisfies and fulfills and many claims about the source of joy and the measure of success. Jesus, however, identifies Himself as the only way to forgiveness and a relationship with God, now and for eternity. Simply put, Jesus is the only way to genuine fulfillment and joy. To help you walk that path, God has given you His Spirit as a guide. Once you name Jesus as your Savior and Lord, His Spirit will lead you in the way you should go. We sinners can't figure out—much less walk—that path on our own. We need to make a conscious decision to follow Jesus as His Spirit guides.

Thus says the LORD, your Redeemer,
   The Holy One of Israel:
   "I am the LORD your God,
   Who teaches you to profit,
   Who leads you by the way you should go."

ISAIAH 48:17

The LORD will guide you continually,
   And satisfy your soul in drought,
   And strengthen your bones;
   You shall be like a watered garden,
   And like a spring of water, whose waters do not
      fail.

ISAIAH 58:11

"When He, the Spirit of truth, has come, He will
guide you into all truth; for He will not speak on His
own authority, but whatever He hears He will speak;
and He will tell you things to come."

JOHN 16:13

Trust in the LORD with all your heart,
   And lean not on your own understanding;
   In all your ways acknowledge Him,
   And He shall direct your paths.

PROVERBS 3:5–6

WISDOM

Wisdom has been defined as "knowledge applied to real life"; godly wisdom is the application of God's truth, as set forth in the Bible, to the everyday challenges and responsibilities of life. God has set forth His truth, His standards, and His commands in the Bible. When you read the Bible, the understanding and knowledge of God you gain are seeds for godly wisdom. Such wisdom will protect you as the world offers options that are very different from what God sets forth as best for you.

"Abide in Me, and I in you. As the branch cannot bear fruit of itself, unless it abides in the vine, neither can you, unless you abide in Me."

JOHN 15:4

My son, if you receive my words,
And treasure my commands within you,
So that you incline your ear to wisdom,
And apply your heart to understanding;
Yes, if you cry out for discernment,
And lift up your voice for understanding,
If you seek her as silver,
And search for her as for hidden treasures;
Then you will understand the fear of the LORD,
And find the knowledge of God.
For the LORD gives wisdom;
From His mouth come knowledge and
understanding;
He stores up sound wisdom for the upright;
He is a shield to those who walk uprightly.

PROVERBS 2:1–7

Get wisdom! Get understanding!
Do not forget, nor turn away from the words of my
mouth.
Do not forsake her, and she will preserve you;
Love her, and she will keep you.
Wisdom is the principal thing;
Therefore get wisdom.
And in all your getting, get understanding.
Exalt her, and she will promote you;
She will bring you honor, when you embrace her.

PROVERBS 4:5–8

ETERNAL GIFT OF HEAVEN

Everyone's soul lives forever. Whether we spend eternity with God (heaven) or away from God (hell) depends on a key decision we make while we are on this earth: Is Jesus Christ who He says He is? Is He the sinless Lamb, whose death on the cross and resurrection from the dead mean forgiveness of sin for those who believe He is God's Son? If you answer yes to those questions, you will be blessed by God's free gift of eternal life with Him.

"My sheep hear My voice, and I know them, and they follow Me. And I give them eternal life, and they shall never perish; neither shall anyone snatch them out of My hand."

JOHN 10:27–28

119

"Most assuredly, I say to you, he who hears My word and believes in Him who sent Me has everlasting life, and shall not come into judgment, but has passed from death into life. Most assuredly, I say to you, the hour is coming, and now is, when the dead will hear the voice of the Son of God; and those who hear will live. For as the Father has life in Himself, so He has granted the Son to have life in Himself."

JOHN 5:24–26

"No one has ascended to heaven but He who came down from heaven, that is, the Son of Man who is in heaven. . . . Whoever believes in Him should not perish but have eternal life. For God so loved the world that He gave His only begotten Son, that whoever believes in Him should not perish but have everlasting life."

JOHN 3:13, 15–16

Having been set free from sin, and having become slaves of God, you have your fruit to holiness, and the end, everlasting life. For the wages of sin is death, but the gift of God is eternal life in Christ Jesus our Lord.

ROMANS 6:22–23

HOLINESS

Holy means "set apart; different; as in different from the world." With that in mind, consider the psalmist's call to God's people to "worship the Lord in the beauty of holiness" (Psalm 29:2). God is gloriously holy, and as His children, we are to live each day reflecting His holiness. We are to live set apart from the world. Our lifestyle is to be distinct from the world's ways for our good and for our holy God's glory.

Let us cleanse ourselves from all filthiness of the flesh and spirit, perfecting holiness in the fear of God.

2 CORINTHIANS 7:1

121

Give to the LORD, O families of the peoples,
Give to the LORD glory and strength.
Give to the LORD the glory due His name;
Bring an offering, and come before Him.
Oh, worship the LORD in the beauty of holiness!

1 CHRONICLES 16:28–29

God did not call us to uncleanness, but in holiness.
Therefore he who rejects this [call to holiness] does
not reject man, but God, who has also given us His
Holy Spirit.

1 THESSALONIANS 4:7–8

Having boldness to enter the Holiest by the blood
of Jesus, by a new and living way which He
consecrated for us, through the veil, that is, His
flesh, and having a High Priest over the house
of God, let us draw near with a true heart in full
assurance of faith, having our hearts sprinkled from
an evil conscience and our bodies washed with pure
water. Let us hold fast the confession of our hope
without wavering, for He who promised is faithful.
And let us consider one another in order to stir up
love and good works.

HEBREWS 10:19–24

GLORIOUS GUARANTEE
OF HIS WORD

God's Word contains glorious promises made by Him who is entirely loving, good, powerful, and wise. When you name Jesus as your Savior, you become a member of God's family, and the Bible's promises become promises for you. Among His many promises to His children, God promises His Holy Spirit, forgiveness of our sin, the righteousness Christ gained for us when He died in our place, guidance for life, hope, relationship with Him, peace, heaven—and the list goes on.

"Let all the house of Israel know assuredly that God has made this Jesus, whom you crucified, both Lord and Christ. . . . Repent, and let every one of you be baptized in the name of Jesus Christ for the remission of sins; and you shall receive the gift of the Holy Spirit. For the promise is to you and to your children, and to all who are afar off, as many as the Lord our God will call."

ACTS 2:36, 38–39

If those who are of the law are heirs, faith is made void and the promise made of no effect, because the law brings about wrath; for where there is no law there is no transgression.

Therefore it is of faith that it might be according to grace, so that the promise might be sure to all the seed, not only to those who are of the law, but also to those who are of the faith of Abraham, who is the father of us all. . . . He did not waver at the promise of God through unbelief, but was strengthened in faith, giving glory to God. . . . And therefore "it was accounted to him for righteousness."

ROMANS 4:14–16, 20, 22

When God made a promise to Abraham, because He could swear by no one greater, He swore by Himself, saying, "Surely blessing I will bless you, and multiplying I will multiply you." And so, after he had patiently endured, he obtained the promise. . . . Thus God, determining to show more abundantly to the heirs of promise the immutability of His counsel, confirmed it by an oath, that by two immutable things, in which it is impossible for God to lie, we might have strong consolation, who have fled for refuge to lay hold of the hope set before us.

HEBREWS 6:13–15, 17–18

The Lord is not slack concerning His promise, as some count slackness, but is longsuffering toward us, not willing that any should perish but that all should come to repentance. . . .

Nevertheless we, according to His promise, look for new heavens and a new earth in which righteousness dwells.

Therefore, beloved, looking forward to these things, be diligent to be found by Him in peace, without spot and blameless.

2 PETER 3:9, 13–14

COVENANT

Our God is a God of covenants. A covenant is an agreement, a contract, a promise. Our God is a promise-making and promise-keeping God. In the Old Testament, for instance, He put a rainbow in the sky as a sign of His promise to never flood the earth again. In the New Testament, God graciously and mercifully covenanted—or promised—to accept His Son's death on the cross as payment for our sins. In response we—by faith—acknowledge both Jesus as God's Son and our need for forgiveness. The blood of Jesus Christ cleanses us from our sin, enables us to be in relationship with our heavenly Father, opens the door to eternity with Him, and seals His promise—or covenant—to be our God now and forever.

"Behold, I send My messenger,
  And he will prepare the way before Me.
  And the Lord, whom you seek,
  Will suddenly come to His temple,
  Even the Messenger of the covenant,
  In whom you delight.
  Behold, He is coming,"
  Says the Lord of hosts.
"But who can endure the day of His coming?
  And who can stand when He appears?
  For He is like a refiner's fire
  And like launderers' soap.
  He will sit as a refiner and a purifier of silver;
  He will purify the sons of Levi,
  And purge them as gold and silver,
  That they may offer to the Lord
  An offering in righteousness."

MALACHI 3:1–3

May the God of peace who brought up our Lord
Jesus from the dead, that great Shepherd of
the sheep, through the blood of the everlasting
covenant, make you complete in every good work
to do His will, working in you what is well pleasing
in His sight, through Jesus Christ, to whom be glory
forever and ever. Amen.

HEBREWS 13:20–21

GOODNESS

References to the goodness of God appear throughout the Bible, and that shouldn't surprise us. After all, what other kind of God would be faithful to us faithless ones? Would any God but a good God be patient with us in our sin, generous in His provision for us, or constant in His love? And God's goodness is not at all weak: He is all-powerful and all-wise as He showers His children with blessings. Even when He doesn't approve of our decisions and actions, even as He waits for us to walk with Him wholeheartedly, our good God provides for us.

Teach me Your way, O Lord,
>And lead me in a smooth path, because of my
>>enemies.
>Do not deliver me to the will of my adversaries;
>For false witnesses have risen against me,
>And such as breathe out violence.
>I would have lost heart, unless I had believed
>That I would see the goodness of the Lord
>In the land of the living.

Wait on the Lord;
>Be of good courage,
>And He shall strengthen your heart;
>Wait, I say, on the Lord!

PSALM 27:11–14

We know that the judgment of God is according to truth against those who practice such things. And do you think this, O man, you who judge those practicing such things, and doing the same, that you will escape the judgment of God? Or do you despise the riches of His goodness, forbearance, and longsuffering, not knowing that the goodness of God leads you to repentance?

ROMANS 2:2–4

HEAVEN

Imagine a place where there is no more death or sorrow or crying or pain. Figuratively speaking, sounds like heaven, doesn't it? Well, according to God's Word, that is literally what heaven is like. The risen Jesus has gone before us to prepare a home for all who name Him as their Lord and Savior, and He waits with open arms for each of us to join Him. To join Him for eternity.

"You shall see heaven open, and the angels of God ascending and descending upon the Son of Man."

JOHN 1:51

We give thanks to the God and Father of our Lord Jesus Christ, praying always for you, since we heard of your faith in Christ Jesus and of your love for all the saints; because of the hope which is laid up for you in heaven, of which you heard before in the word of the truth of the gospel, which has come to you, as it has also in all the world, and is bringing forth fruit, as it is also among you since the day you heard and knew the grace of God in truth.

COLOSSIANS 1:3–6

"Heaven is My throne,
And earth is My footstool.
Where is the house that you will build Me?
And where is the place of My rest?
For all those things My hand has made,
And all those things exist,"
Says the LORD.
"But on this one will I look:
On him who is poor and of a contrite spirit,
And who trembles at My word."

ISAIAH 66:1–2

"I am the bread of life. He who comes to Me shall never hunger, and he who believes in Me shall never thirst. But I said to you that you have seen Me and yet do not believe. All that the Father gives Me will come to Me, and the one who comes to Me I will by no means cast out. For I have come down from heaven, not to do My own will, but the will of Him who sent Me. This is the will of the Father who sent Me, that of all He has given Me I should lose nothing, but should raise it up at the last day. And this is the will of Him who sent Me, that everyone who sees the Son and believes in Him may have everlasting life; and I will raise him up at the last day."

JOHN 6:35–40

GOD
PROMISES
TO . . .

BE YOUR SALVATION

Only one invitation in life—and your decision about whether to accept it—will affect you forever. That is God's invitation to believe that Jesus is His Son, the sinless God-man who came to earth to die. Jesus was the unblemished sacrificial Lamb whose shed blood covers all of humanity's sins—all of *your* sins—past, present, and future. If you believe this to be the gospel truth—which it absolutely is—you are saved forever from the consequences of your sins. Those consequences would be separation from Holy God and an eternity in hell. Do you believe in your heart that God raised Jesus from the dead? And have you publically declared your commitment to Jesus? If so, you know salvation: you know forgiveness, membership in God's family, and the absolute certainty of eternity in heaven.

If you confess with your mouth the Lord Jesus and believe in your heart that God has raised Him from the dead, you will be saved. For with the heart one believes unto righteousness, and with the mouth confession is made unto salvation. For the Scripture says, "Whoever believes on Him will not be put to shame." For there is no distinction between Jew and Greek, for the same Lord over all is rich to all who call upon Him. For "whoever calls on the name of the LORD shall be saved."

ROMANS 10:9–13

By grace you have been saved through faith, and that not of yourselves; it is the gift of God, not of works, lest anyone should boast. For we are His workmanship, created in Christ Jesus for good works, which God prepared beforehand that we should walk in them.

EPHESIANS 2:8–10

"For God so loved the world that He gave His only begotten Son, that whoever believes in Him should not perish but have everlasting life. For God did not send His Son into the world to condemn the world, but that the world through Him might be saved."

JOHN 3:16–17

BE YOUR REWARD

H ere it is in black and white: you can do noth-
ing to earn or merit or deserve God's love, His
forgiveness, or a reservation in heaven. Your salva-
tion is pure grace; it is purely a gift from God. We
respond to that indescribable gift by loving God—by
obeying His commands; by serving Him, our fam-
ily and friends, people in our neighborhood and the
workplace, people in the church and in the world; by
being faithful stewards of the talents, abilities, oppor-
tunities, and blessings He bestows; and by sharing
the good news of Jesus. Heaven is a sure thing for
believers; the rewards that await us there depend on
how we live.

Behold, the Lord God shall come with a strong hand,
    And His arm shall rule for Him;
    Behold, His reward is with Him,
    and His work before Him.
    He will feed His flock like a shepherd;
    He will gather the lambs with His arm,
    And carry them in His bosom,
    And gently lead those who are with young.

ISAIAH 40:10–11

The fear of the Lord is clean, enduring forever;
    The judgments of the Lord are true and righteous
        altogether.
    More to be desired are they than gold,
    Yea, than much fine gold;
    Sweeter also than honey and the honeycomb.
    Moreover by them Your servant is warned,
    And in keeping them there is great reward.

PSALM 19:9–11

Now he who plants and he who waters are one, and
each one will receive his own reward according to
his own labor.

1 CORINTHIANS 3:8

BE YOUR ENCOURAGEMENT

God's Holy Spirit strengthens believers and enriches our lives in wonderful ways. The Spirit is our Teacher when we study the Bible. He enables us to learn, to memorize, and, later, to recall verses and truths from God's Word. The Spirit is our Guide in life, and He is the Comforter and Encourager during life's inevitable hard times. And the Spirit prays for us when we aren't sure how to pray or when we are too tired, too beaten down, to pray. May these truths about the Spirit of God, the Source of power in a believer's life, give you hope and encourage you to live as God's child.

I am not ashamed of the gospel of Christ, for it is the power of God to salvation for everyone who believes, for the Jew first and also for the Greek. For in it the righteousness of God is revealed from faith to faith; as it is written, "The just shall live by faith."

ROMANS 1:16–17

Because Your lovingkindness is better than life,
My lips shall praise You.
Thus I will bless You while I live;
I will lift up my hands in Your name.
My soul shall be satisfied as with marrow
and fatness,
And my mouth shall praise You with joyful lips.

PSALM 63:3–5

The Lord is your keeper;
The Lord is your shade at your right hand.
The sun shall not strike you by day,
Nor the moon by night. . . .
The Lord shall preserve your going out and your
coming in
From this time forth, and even forevermore.

PSALM 121:5–6, 8

GOD PROMISES TO . . .

BE YOUR JOY

Anyone can be happy when the test results are good, the bills get paid, and the kids obey. But only people who know Jesus can know joy when the test results are bad, not all the bills can be paid this month, and the kids rebel. Joy is not based on the fleeting circumstances of a specific day; joy is based on Jesus' victory over sin and death and on the promise of spending eternity with Him. May the comfort of the Spirit, the big-picture perspective on today's problems in light of an eternal heaven, and the confidence that our wise and loving Sovereign God is in control always be reasons for joy!

"If you keep My commandments, you will abide in My love, just as I have kept My Father's commandments and abide in His love.

"These things I have spoken to you, that My joy may remain in you, and that your joy may be full."

JOHN 15:10–11

Rejoice in the Lord always. Again I will say, rejoice!

Let your gentleness be known to all men. The Lord is at hand.

PHILIPPIANS 4:4–5

Yet I will rejoice in the Lord,
I will joy in the God of my salvation.
The Lord God is my strength;
He will make my feet like deer's feet,
And He will make me walk on my high hills.

HABAKKUK 3:18–19

I rejoiced greatly when brethren came and testified of the truth that is in you, just as you walk in the truth. I have no greater joy than to hear that my children walk in truth.

3 JOHN vv. 3–4

GOD PROMISES TO . . .

BE YOUR REASON FOR PRAISE AND WORSHIP

According to the classic seventeenth-century Westminster Confession, God created human beings to glorify Him and enjoy Him forever. When we wholeheartedly worship God, we do both: We glorify God when we sing and shout His praises, when we celebrate who He is in all His magnificence, when we thank Him for His love made manifest in our lives in countless ways. And maybe during a time of worship you have found yourself truly enjoying the time with your God. You may even sense that you are doing exactly what God created you to do. If you haven't experienced such a moment—or you haven't in a while—keep worshipping!

While I live I will praise the LORD;
   I will sing praises to my God while I have
      my being.

PSALM 146:2

The LORD is the great God,
   And the great King above all gods.
   In His hand are the deep places of the earth;
   The heights of the hills are His also.
   The sea is His, for He made it;
   And His hands formed the dry land.
Oh come, let us worship and bow down;
   Let us kneel before the LORD our Maker.

PSALM 95:3–6

The poor shall eat and be satisfied;
   Those who seek Him will praise the LORD.
   Let your heart live forever!
All the ends of the world
   Shall remember and turn to the LORD,
   And all the families of the nations
   Shall worship before You.

PSALM 22:26–27

I will praise You, O Lord, with my whole heart;
 I will tell of all Your marvelous works.
 I will be glad and rejoice in You;
 I will sing praise to Your name, O Most High.

PSALM 9:1–2

I will bless the Lord at all times;
 His praise shall continually be in my mouth.
 My soul shall make its boast in the Lord;
 The humble shall hear of it and be glad.
 Oh, magnify the Lord with me,
 And let us exalt His name together.

PSALM 34:1–3

Give to the Lord, O families of the peoples,
 Give to the Lord glory and strength.
 Give to the Lord the glory due His name;
 Bring an offering, and come before Him.
 Oh, worship the Lord in the beauty of holiness!

1 CHRONICLES 16:28–29

BE YOUR COURAGE

It's definitely no coincidence that the message "Fear not" appears hundreds of times in the Bible. Clearly God is aware that this world gives His people much to fear—and He doesn't want fear to haunt us, much less immobilize us. So He encourages you with reminders that He is always with you, that He will never forsake you, and that nothing will ever be able to separate you from His love for you. So be encouraged—and fear not!

Wait on the LORD;
    Be of good courage,
    And He shall strengthen your heart;
    Wait, I say, on the LORD!

PSALM 27:14

"Be strong and of good courage, do not fear nor be afraid of them; for the LORD your God, He is the One who goes with you. He will not leave you nor forsake you."

Then Moses called Joshua and said to him in the sight of all Israel, "Be strong and of good courage, for you must go with this people to the land which the LORD has sworn to their fathers to give them, and you shall cause them to inherit it."

DEUTERONOMY 31:6–7

"Be strong and of good courage, for to this people you shall divide as an inheritance the land which I swore to their fathers to give them. Only be strong and very courageous, that you may observe to do according to all the law which Moses My servant commanded you; do not turn from it to the right hand or to the left, that you may prosper wherever you go. This Book of the Law shall not depart from your mouth, but you shall meditate in it day and night, that you may observe to do according to all that is written in it. For then you will make your way prosperous, and then you will have good success."

JOSHUA 1:6–8

GOD PROMISES TO . . .

FILL YOUR HEART

Your relationship with Jesus is a matter of the heart. That life-giving relationship has nothing to do with how many times you pray during your waking hours, how many verses (chapters?) of the Bible you've memorized, or how much of your paycheck goes into the offering plate. Your relationship with Jesus is a matter of loving Him with all you are, of making Him most important in your life, of being willing to serve Him instead of doing what you want to do. Your relationship is a matter of having His Spirit show you your sin and then confessing that sin so, forgiven, you can once again enjoy your friendship with Jesus.

Search me, O God, and know my heart;
  Try me, and know my anxieties;
  And see if there is any wicked way in me,
  And lead me in the way everlasting.

PSALM 139:23–24

With my whole heart I have sought You;
  Oh, let me not wander from Your commandments!
  Your word I have hidden in my heart,
  That I might not sin against You.
  Blessed are You, O LORD!
  Teach me Your statutes.

PSALM 119:10–12

Praise the LORD!
I will praise the LORD with my whole heart,
  In the assembly of the upright and in the
    congregation.
The works of the LORD are great,
  Studied by all who have pleasure in them.
  His work is honorable and glorious,
  And His righteousness endures forever.
  He has made His wonderful works to be
    remembered;
  The LORD is gracious and full of compassion.

PSALM 111:1–4

BE YOUR INHERITANCE

As a child of God—and that's what you are once you named Jesus as your Savior and Lord—you have an amazing and eternal inheritance awaiting you. That inheritance is eternal life in God's presence: an eternity in heaven, an eternity of seeing Jesus face-to-face, an eternity without sadness or pain. That inheritance cannot be taken away from you, and that inheritance will never fade. What amazing grace! What amazing love!

The LORD knows the days of the upright,
    And their inheritance shall be forever.
    They shall not be ashamed in the evil time,
    And in the days of famine they shall be satisfied.

PSALM 37:18–19

O Lᴏʀᴅ, You are the portion of my inheritance and
        my cup;
  You maintain my lot.
  The lines have fallen to me in pleasant places;
  Yes, I have a good inheritance.
I will bless the Lᴏʀᴅ who has given me counsel;
  My heart also instructs me in the night seasons.

PSALM 16:5–7

Oh, clap your hands, all you peoples!
  Shout to God with the voice of triumph!
  For the Lᴏʀᴅ Most High is awesome;
  He is a great King over all the earth.
  He will subdue the peoples under us,
  And the nations under our feet.
  He will choose our inheritance for us,
  The excellence of Jacob whom He loves.

PSALM 47:1–4

[Give] thanks to the Father who has qualified us
to be partakers of the inheritance of the saints in
the light. He has delivered us from the power of
darkness and conveyed us into the kingdom of
the Son of His love, in whom we have redemption
through His blood, the forgiveness of sins.

COLOSSIANS 1:12–14

BE YOUR LIGHT

A candle in the dark night of a power outage . . .
A flashlight in a cave . . . A word of truth in a
world of lies and spin and propaganda. . . . As each
of these scenarios suggests, a little light can have a
huge impact on a situation. Similarly, you who love
Jesus can't help but shine with His light. Don't try
to cover it up! Let it shine. And as that light shines,
you can't help but impact your world. That light in the
darkness not only gives God glory but also attracts
people who don't yet know Jesus.

"I am the light of the world. He who follows Me shall
not walk in darkness, but have the light of life."

JOHN 8:12

In the beginning was the Word, and the Word was with God, and the Word was God. He was in the beginning with God. All things were made through Him, and without Him nothing was made that was made. In Him was life, and the life was the light of men. And the light shines in the darkness, and the darkness did not comprehend it.

There was a man sent from God, whose name was John. This man came for a witness, to bear witness of the Light, that all through him might believe. He was not that Light, but was sent to bear witness of that Light. That was the true Light which gives light to every man coming into the world.

JOHN 1:1–9

"You are the light of the world. A city that is set on a hill cannot be hidden. Nor do they light a lamp and put it under a basket, but on a lampstand, and it gives light to all who are in the house. Let your light so shine before men, that they may see your good works and glorify your Father in heaven."

MATTHEW 5:14–16

BE YOUR HEART'S DESIRE

Our God is a loving God, but He isn't a Santa Claus. Our God loves to give good gifts, but in His economy the best gifts are not tangible or material. Our God feels compassion when we hurt, but He does allow hardships that will refine our character and strengthen our faith. Against the backdrop of these truths, we can better understand the often misunderstood statement that God will give us the desires of our heart. The promise is that, as you pray, read His Word, and grow closer to the Lord, He will change your heart so that what you desire for yourself is what He desires for you. A wonderful result of that heart change will be a richer relationship with Him.

Behold, I was brought forth in iniquity,
And in sin my mother conceived me.
Behold, You desire truth in the inward parts,
And in the hidden part You will make me to know
wisdom.

PSALM 51:5–6

Whom have I in heaven but You?
And there is none upon earth that I desire
besides You.
My flesh and my heart fail;
But God is the strength of my heart and my
portion forever.

PSALM 73:25–26

You open Your hand
And satisfy the desire of every living thing.
The Lord is righteous in all His ways,
Gracious in all His works.
The Lord is near to all who call upon Him,
To all who call upon Him in truth.

PSALM 145:16–18

BE YOUR EXAMPLE OF SERVANTHOOD

Jesus was not the king that God's people of His day expected. They were looking for power and might, for one whose leadership would mean deliverance from the tyranny of Rome. But Jesus came to serve. The One who washed the feet of His disciples when they were too prideful to volunteer for the task, the One who gave His life on the cross so that we sinners would not spend eternity apart from God, came with a different kind of power and might. Jesus came to show the world a love it never would have imagined, a love that delivered us from the tyranny of sin and death. When you follow Jesus' example and serve others, your obedience will mean the blessing of a Christlike heart and Christlike joy.

"Israel, what does the Lord your God require of you, but to fear the Lord your God, to walk in all His ways and to love Him, to serve the Lord your God with all your heart and with all your soul."

DEUTERONOMY 10:12

From the Lord you will receive the reward of the inheritance; for you serve the Lord Christ.

COLOSSIANS 3:24

Make a joyful shout to the Lord, all you lands!
   Serve the Lord with gladness;
   Come before His presence with singing.
   Know that the Lord, He is God;
   It is He who has made us, and not we ourselves;
   We are His people and the sheep of His pasture.
Enter into His gates with thanksgiving,
   And into His courts with praise.
   Be thankful to Him, and bless His name.
   For the Lord is good;
   His mercy is everlasting,
   And His truth endures to all generations.

PSALM 100:1–5

BE YOUR REASON FOR HUMILITY

It may be counterintuitive; it's definitely counter-cultural. "It" is humility, the willingness not to exalt self but to exalt others; the choice to care about other people's needs and not just our own. Humility is an awareness of our sinfulness as well as our weaknesses and limitations. As such, humility can move us closer to Jesus with a heart ready to receive all that He wants to give. Peace, direction, comfort, love, close fellowship with Him—humble yourself and know such precious blessings from God.

By humility and the fear of the LORD
  Are riches and honor and life.

PROVERBS 22:4

For thus says the High and Lofty One
Who inhabits eternity, whose name is Holy:
"I dwell in the high and holy place,
With him who has a contrite and humble spirit,
To revive the spirit of the humble,
And to revive the heart of the contrite ones."

ISAIAH 57:15

"God resists the proud,
But gives grace to the humble."
Therefore submit to God. Resist the devil and he will
flee from you. Draw near to God and He will draw
near to you. Cleanse your hands, you sinners; and
purify your hearts, you double-minded.

JAMES 4:6–8

The LORD lifts up the humble;
He casts the wicked down to the ground.
Sing to the LORD with thanksgiving;
Sing praises on the harp to our God,
Who covers the heavens with clouds,
Who prepares rain for the earth,
Who makes grass to grow on the mountains.

PSALM 147:6–8

GOD PROMISES TO . . .

BE YOUR FRIEND

What do you value in a friend? Loyalty? Integrity? Trust? A good friend is willing to listen to your pain, to rejoice when you rejoice, and to pray for you in every season of life. A good friend brings the best out of you. A good friend knows you well and loves you anyway. Whatever traits you want in a friend—this list of qualities included—you will find existing perfectly in Jesus. He truly is the best Friend you will ever have.

A man who has friends must himself be friendly,
But there is a friend who sticks closer than
a brother.

PROVERBS 18:24

Do you see that faith was working together with his works, and by works faith was made perfect? And the Scripture was fulfilled which says, "Abraham believed God, and it was accounted to him for righteousness." And he was called the friend of God. You see then that a man is justified by works, and not by faith only.

JAMES 2:22–24

"Greater love has no one than this, than to lay down one's life for his friends. You are My friends if you do whatever I command you. No longer do I call you servants, for a servant does not know what his master is doing; but I have called you friends, for all things that I heard from My Father I have made known to you."

JOHN 15:13–15

[Jehoshaphat] said: "O Lord God of our fathers, are You not God in heaven, and do You not rule over all the kingdoms of the nations, and in Your hand is there not power and might, so that no one is able to withstand You? Are You not our God, who drove out the inhabitants of this land before Your people Israel, and gave it to the descendants of Abraham Your friend forever?"

2 CHRONICLES 20:6–7

GOD PROMISES TO . . .

BE YOUR HOPE

In everyday conversation, hope often means no more than wishful thinking. A follower of Christ, however, lives with a different kind of hope, a hope that is sure, guaranteed, and life-giving. Believers hope with confident expectation that God has completely and permanently overcome darkness, sin, and death. We know God as Promise-Maker and Promise-Keeper: we see His track record in the Bible, and we can undoubtedly look back on our own life and see evidence of His faithfulness and love. Our hope is solid: our God does all that He says He will do.

You are my hope, O Lord God;
    You are my trust from my youth.

PSALM 71:5

We give thanks to God always for you all, . . . remembering without ceasing your work of faith, labor of love, and patience of hope in our Lord Jesus Christ.

1 THESSALONIANS 1:2–33

Blessed be the God and Father of our Lord Jesus Christ, who according to His abundant mercy has begotten us again to a living hope through the resurrection of Jesus Christ from the dead, to an inheritance incorruptible and undefiled and that does not fade away, reserved in heaven for you.

1 PETER 1:3–4

Having been justified by faith, we have peace with God through our Lord Jesus Christ, through whom also we have access by faith into this grace in which we stand, and rejoice in hope of the glory of God. . . . Now hope does not disappoint, because the love of God has been poured out in our hearts by the Holy Spirit who was given to us.

ROMANS 5:1–2, 5

O Israel, hope in the LORD;
  For with the LORD there is mercy,
  And with Him is abundant redemption.

PSALM 130:7

I, therefore, the prisoner of the Lord, beseech you to walk worthy of the calling with which you were called, with all lowliness and gentleness, with longsuffering, bearing with one another in love, endeavoring to keep the unity of the Spirit in the bond of peace. There is one body and one Spirit, just as you were called in one hope of your calling; one Lord, one faith, one baptism; one God and Father of all, who is above all, and through all, and in you all.

EPHESIANS 4:1–6

BE WORTHY OF YOUR TRUST

Maybe you've heard the story of the tightrope walker who walked across Niagara Falls. Sure and steady, he went over, and then—again sure and steady—he walked back. What an impressive performance! Awe-inspiring—but not entirely confidence-inspiring. He had no takers when he offered to carry someone from the crowd across the falls. Trust isn't just marveling at the good and gracious acts of our God: trust is putting every aspect of your life into His care despite the risks, the threats, the unknowns, the fears. Have you done that?

But let all those rejoice who put their trust in You;
    Let them ever shout for joy, because You defend
        them;
    Let those also who love Your name
    Be joyful in You.
    For You, O Lord, will bless the righteous;
    With favor You will surround him as with a shield.

                PSALM 5:11–12

The Lord is my rock and my fortress and my
        deliverer;
    My God, my strength, in whom I will trust;
    My shield and the horn of my salvation, my
        stronghold.
    I will call upon the Lord, who is worthy to be
        praised;
    So shall I be saved from my enemies.

                PSALM 18:2–3

Trust in the Lord with all your heart,
    And lean not on your own understanding;
    In all your ways acknowledge Him,
    And He shall direct your paths.

                PROVERBS 3:5–6

GOD PROMISES TO . . .

HEAR YOU WHEN YOU PRAY

Twenty-four/seven access to the Creator of the universe, the Author of history, the Victor over sin and death, the sovereign, gracious, good, wise, compassionate God! That's a privilege that comes when you name Jesus as your Savior and Lord. Forgiven for your sin, you can approach the holy God and talk to Him about anything and everything that is on your heart and mind. Challenge yourself to learn to have an ongoing conversation with your God as you walk through each day—and remember that a conversation involves listening too!

"Call to Me, and I will answer you, and show you great and mighty things, which you do not know."

JEREMIAH 33:3

"If My people who are called by My name will humble themselves, and pray and seek My face, and turn from their wicked ways, then I will hear from heaven, and will forgive their sin and heal their land."

2 CHRONICLES 7:14

Hear my prayer, O LORD,
    And let my cry come to You.
    Do not hide Your face from me in the day of my
        trouble;
    Incline Your ear to me;
    In the day that I call, answer me speedily.

PSALM 102:1–2

Be anxious for nothing, but in everything by prayer and supplication, with thanksgiving, let your requests be made known to God; and the peace of God, which surpasses all understanding, will guard your hearts and minds through Christ Jesus.

PHILIPPIANS 4:6–7

"And whenever you stand praying, if you have anything against anyone, forgive him, that your Father in heaven may also forgive you your trespasses."

MARK 11:25

MAKE YOUR LIFE SPIRITUALLY FRUITFUL

God's Word teaches that the world will know who His people are because of the way we love, but love is just one fruit of a life dedicated to Jesus. The presence of the Holy Spirit in God's people means the additional fruit of joy, peace, patience, kindness, goodness, faithfulness, gentleness, and self-control. Such traits are evidence of the life-transforming work God's Spirit does to make His people—to make you—more like Jesus Christ.

"These are the [seeds] sown on good ground, those who hear the word, accept it, and bear fruit: some thirtyfold, some sixty, and some a hundred."

MARK 4:20

"I am the vine, you are the branches. He who abides in Me, and I in him, bears much fruit; for without Me you can do nothing. If anyone does not abide in Me, he is cast out as a branch and is withered; and they gather them and throw them into the fire, and they are burned. If you abide in Me, and My words abide in you, you will ask what you desire, and it shall be done for you."

JOHN 15:5–7

The fruit of the Spirit is love, joy, peace, longsuffering, kindness, goodness, faithfulness, gentleness, self-control. Against such there is no law. And those who are Christ's have crucified the flesh with its passions and desires. If we live in the Spirit, let us also walk in the Spirit. Let us not become conceited, provoking one another, envying one another.

GALATIANS 5:22–26

"You did not choose Me, but I chose you and appointed you that you should go and bear fruit, and that your fruit should remain, that whatever you ask the Father in My name He may give you."

JOHN 15:16

LOVE AND DELIGHT IN YOU

Y ou may be blessed to have a parent, a spouse, or a friend who delights in you, who seems to love everything about you, and who enjoys simply being with you. What a source of joy! Did you know that the Almighty God, your Creator, delights in you as well? And the longer you walk with Him and the more closely you walk with Him, the greater will be your delight in Him!

"Let him who glories glory in this,
　　That he understands and knows Me,
　　That I am the LORD, exercising lovingkindness,
　　　　judgment, and righteousness in the earth.
　　For in these I delight," says the LORD.

JEREMIAH 9:24

Blessed is the man
Who walks not in the counsel of the ungodly,
    Nor stands in the path of sinners,
    Nor sits in the seat of the scornful;
But his delight is in the law of the LORD,
    And in His law he meditates day and night.
He shall be like a tree
    Planted by the rivers of water,
    That brings forth its fruit in its season,
    Whose leaf also shall not wither;
And whatever he does shall prosper.

PSALM 1:1–3

"If you turn away your foot from the Sabbath,
    From doing your pleasure on My holy day,
    And call the Sabbath a delight,
    The holy day of the LORD honorable,
    And shall honor Him, not doing your own ways,
    Nor finding your own pleasure,
    Nor speaking your own words,
    Then you shall delight yourself in the LORD;
    And I will cause you to ride on the high hills
        of the earth,
    And feed you with the heritage of Jacob
        your father."

ISAIAH 58:13–14

BE YOUR SACRIFICE

Jesus came to earth knowing that His purpose was to die for the sins of humanity, for your sin. As the moment for His crucifixion neared, the reality of what His sacrificial death on the cross would mean had Him begging His heavenly Father to keep Him from experiencing that indescribable physical pain and, worse, the spiritual agony of being separated from God for three days. During your time on this earth, your sacrifices for others will probably not be so public or so physically painful; your sacrifices definitely won't be as spiritually painful as Jesus' because you won't be separated from God. Still, your prayers may echo Jesus' prayer: "I don't want to do this—but I do want to do what You want me to do, God." And just as God enabled Jesus to serve sacrificially, He will enable you.

Be imitators of God as dear children. And walk in love, as Christ also has loved us and given Himself for us, an offering and a sacrifice to God for a sweet-smelling aroma.

EPHESIANS 5:1–2

Christ has not entered the holy places made with hands, which are copies of the true, but into heaven itself, now to appear in the presence of God for us; not that He should offer Himself often, as the high priest enters the Most Holy Place every year with blood of another—He then would have had to suffer often since the foundation of the world; but now, once at the end of the ages, He has appeared to put away sin by the sacrifice of Himself.

HEBREWS 9:24–26

Let us continually offer the sacrifice of praise to God, that is, the fruit of our lips, giving thanks to His name. But do not forget to do good and to share, for with such sacrifices God is well pleased.

HEBREWS 13:15–16

GOD'S UNCONDITIONAL LOVE IS *with* YOU WHEN YOU . . .

TALK TO HIM ABOUT YOUR PROBLEMS

Think about the list of "Favorites" in your phone. The people listed there are probably the first you call when something good or something bad happens, when you need to talk, be prayed for, or be counseled. Do you turn to Jesus as your last resort? May that default change as you grow in your knowledge of, love for, and closeness to Jesus.

Both riches and honor come from You,
And You reign over all.
In Your hand is power and might;
In Your hand it is to make great
And to give strength to all.

1 CHRONICLES 29:12

"With men this is impossible, but with God all things are possible."

MATTHEW 19:26

"For the eyes of the Lord are on the righteous,
And His ears are open to their prayers;
But the face of the Lord is against those who do evil."
And who is he who will harm you if you become followers of what is good? But even if you should suffer for righteousness' sake, you are blessed.

1 PETER 3:12–14

We had the sentence of death in ourselves, that we should not trust in ourselves but in God who raises the dead, who delivered us from so great a death, and does deliver us; in whom we trust that He will still deliver us.

2 CORINTHIANS 1:9–10

RELY ON HIM TO GUIDE YOUR LIFE

Maybe you've heard this observation made: in the land of the blind, the one-eyed man is king. Even someone just a little bit more capable than we are—whether in knowledge, experience, wisdom, or the simple ability to see—can be a huge help as we journey through life. We who are blessed to be God's children, however, are blessed to have Someone far more capable than we are—God Himself—accompanying, guiding, and assisting us on this journey of life.

"Fear not, for I am with you;
   Be not dismayed, for I am your God.
   I will strengthen you,
   Yes, I will help you,
   I will uphold you with My righteous right hand."

ISAIAH 41:10

178

"I will go before you
And make the crooked places straight;
I will break in pieces the gates of bronze
And cut the bars of iron.
I will give you the treasures of darkness
And hidden riches of secret places,
That you may know that I, the LORD,
Who call you by your name,
Am the God of Israel."

ISAIAH 45:2–3

"For the mountains shall depart
And the hills be removed,
But My kindness shall not depart from you,
Nor shall My covenant of peace be removed,"
Says the LORD, who has mercy on you.

ISAIAH 54:10

I will sing of Your power;
Yes, I will sing aloud of Your mercy in the morning;
For You have been my defense
And refuge in the day of my trouble.
To You, O my Strength, I will sing praises;
For God is my defense,
My God of mercy.

PSALM 59:16–17

SHARE YOUR BLESSINGS WITH OTHERS

Your time, your talents, your finances—anything and everything that God has blessed you with—provide you with opportunities to help believers and non-believers alike. God encourages His people to generously share and serve using all that He gives us. So choose to make yourself and your resources available to God. He will use you and all that you offer Him to bless others, and as you do so, you will be giving God glory.

"You shall surely give to him, and your heart should not be grieved when you give to him, because for this thing the Lord your God will bless you in all your works and in all to which you put your hand. For the poor will never cease from the land; therefore I command you, saying, 'You shall open your hand wide to your brother, to your poor and your needy, in your land.'"

DEUTERONOMY 15:10–11

"The Lord makes poor and makes rich;
    He brings low and lifts up.
    He raises the poor from the dust
    and lifts the beggar from the ash heap,
    to set them among princes
    and make them inherit the throne of glory.
For the pillars of the earth are the Lord's,
    and He has set the world upon them."

1 SAMUEL 2:7–8

"Give, and it will be given to you: good measure, pressed down, shaken together, and running over will be put into your bosom. For with the same measure that you use, it will be measured back to you."

LUKE 6:38

PRAY WITH YOUR LOVED ONES

At best, on this side of heaven, we can have only a vague idea of the power and the efficacy of our prayers. God calls us to pray constantly about anything, any person, any situation that concerns us. Even before we do, our good and gracious God is at work in the situation for the good of people involved and for His glory. Pray *with* loved ones; pray *for* loved ones. Pray with confidence in God and His good plans. Pray with the expectation that God is at work for the good of the people involved, for growth in their relationship with Him, and for His glory that others might see and pursue Him.

The Lord is near to all who call upon Him,
   To all who call upon Him in truth.
   He will fulfill the desire of those who fear Him;
   He also will hear their cry and save them.

PSALM 145:18–19

Rejoice in the Lord always. Again I will say, rejoice!
   Let your gentleness be known to all men. The Lord is at hand.
   Be anxious for nothing, but in everything by prayer and supplication, with thanksgiving, let your requests be made known to God; and the peace of God, which surpasses all understanding, will guard your hearts and minds through Christ Jesus.

PHILIPPIANS 4:4–7

Seeing then that we have a great High Priest who has passed through the heavens, Jesus the Son of God, let us hold fast our confession. . . . Let us therefore come boldly to the throne of grace, that we may obtain mercy and find grace to help in time of need.

HEBREWS 4:14, 16

GOD'S UNCONDITIONAL LOVE IS WITH
YOU WHEN YOU . . .

TRY TO HONOR HIM
WITH YOUR LIFE

To be dedicated is to be set apart for a specific purpose or honor. To dedicate one's life to God means having a new purpose in life: serving Him, sharing the truth of Jesus, loving others. And the opportunity to dedicate your life to God is in itself an honor. Here's something to think about—not to beat yourself up about, but just to think about. If someone looked at you—if that person looked at your calendar, your checkbook register, your home, your use of your time—what evidence would he see that you are dedicated to Jesus?

"Most assuredly, I say to you, he who believes in Me, the works that I do he will do also; and greater works than these he will do, because I go to My Father. And whatever you ask in My name, that I will do, that the Father may be glorified in the Son. If you ask anything in My name, I will do it."

JOHN 14:12–14

"In that day you will ask Me nothing. Most assuredly, I say to you, whatever you ask the Father in My name He will give you. Until now you have asked nothing in My name. Ask, and you will receive, that your joy may be full."

JOHN 16:23–24

I will greatly rejoice in the LORD,
My soul shall be joyful in my God;
For He has clothed me with the garments of
salvation,
He has covered me with the robe of righteousness,
As a bridegroom decks himself with ornaments,
And as a bride adorns herself with her jewels.
For as the earth brings forth its bud,
As the garden causes the things that are sown in
it to spring forth,
So the Lord GOD will cause righteousness and
praise to spring forth before all the nations.

ISAIAH 61:10–11

WAIT PATIENTLY FOR HIM TO ANSWER YOUR PRAYERS

When tragedy strikes, when the loss is unexpected, when the situation we thought was improving takes a sudden downturn—will we look for God to do good in those circumstances, in the hearts of the people involved, in our own lives? Will we be confident that God will do what is loving and right, just and redemptive? Will we trust God? The choice is ours just as it's always been the choice of God's people. Be encouraged by the voices of these fellow believers.

Every word of God is pure;
   He is a shield to those who put their trust in Him.

PROVERBS 30:5

My soul, wait silently for God alone,
  For my expectation is from Him.
  He only is my rock and my salvation;
  He is my defense;
  I shall not be moved.
  In God is my salvation and my glory;
  The rock of my strength,
  And my refuge, is in God.
Trust in Him at all times, you people;
  Pour out your heart before Him;
  God is a refuge for us.

PSALM 62:5–8

"I am the Lord, and there is no other;
  There is no God besides Me.
  I will gird you, though you have not known Me,
  That they may know from the rising of the sun to
      its setting
  That there is none besides Me.
  I am the Lord, and there is no other."

ISAIAH 45:5–6

Do not be deceived, my beloved brethren. Every
good gift and every perfect gift is from above, and
comes down from the Father of lights, with whom
there is no variation or shadow of turning.

JAMES 1:16–17

MAKE JESUS YOUR TOP PRIORITY

Recognizing your sin, accepting Jesus' death on the cross on your behalf, and deciding to live with Him as your Savior and Lord mark the beginning of your life as a Christian. That life becomes richer and more significant when you invest time and energy in knowing Jesus better. Key to that kind of growth is studying God's Word, spending time in prayer, and becoming involved in a good Bible-believing church. Doing so will mean saying no to other activities, but you will never regret having as your number one priority in life getting to know Jesus better.

Teach me, O Lord, the way of Your statutes,
    And I shall keep it to the end.
    Give me understanding, and I shall keep Your law;
    Indeed, I shall observe it with my whole heart.
    Make me walk in the path of Your commandments,
    For I delight in it.

PSALM 119:33–35

Beloved, let us cleanse ourselves from all filthiness
of the flesh and spirit, perfecting holiness in the fear
of God.

2 CORINTHIANS 7:1

Your word is a lamp to my feet
    And a light to my path.
    I have sworn and confirmed
    That I will keep Your righteous judgments.
    I am afflicted very much;
    Revive me, O Lord, according to Your word.
    Accept, I pray, the freewill offerings of my mouth,
        O Lord,
    And teach me Your judgments.
    My life is continually in my hand,
    Yet I do not forget Your law.

PSALM 119:105–109

CONFESS YOUR SINS AND ASK HIS FORGIVENESS

A huge canyon exists between our holy God and us sinners. Jesus' death on the cross provided a bridge across that canyon. Our confession of our sin is our walking across that bridge and into the presence of our loving and forgiving God. You can be absolutely sure that He will forgive you, so don't hesitate to confess your sins. In fact, make confession part of your daily prayer so that nothing stands between you and your heavenly Father.

"I will be merciful to their unrighteousness, and their sins and their lawless deeds I will remember no more."

HEBREWS 8:12

The Lord is far from the wicked,

But He hears the prayer of the righteous.

The light of the eyes rejoices the heart,

And a good report makes the bones healthy.

The ear that hears the rebukes of life

Will abide among the wise.

He who disdains instruction despises his own soul,

But he who heeds rebuke gets understanding.

The fear of the Lord is the instruction of wisdom,

And before honor is humility.

PROVERBS 15:29–33

Let the wicked forsake his way,

And the unrighteous man his thoughts;

Let him return to the Lord,

And He will have mercy on him;

And to our God,

For He will abundantly pardon.

ISAIAH 55:7

To the praise of the glory of His grace . . . [God] made us accepted in the Beloved [Jesus].

In Him we have redemption through His blood, the forgiveness of sins, according to the riches of His grace.

EPHESIANS 1:6–7

TALK ABOUT JESUS WITH PEOPLE WHO DON'T KNOW HIM

Jesus has commanded every one of His follow-ers—those who heard His voice in Jerusalem and those of us who have heard His voice through the pages of Scripture—to share the good news of His sacrificial death for people's sin, His resurrec-tion from the dead, and the forgiveness of sin that is available to all. Talking about your relationship with Jesus—also referred to as "sharing your Christian faith"—is the responsibility of every follower of Christ. Know that the Holy Spirit will give you words to say when you step out in faith and in obedience to this command.

I am not ashamed of the gospel of Christ, for it is the power of God to salvation for everyone who believes, for the Jew first and also for the Greek.

ROMANS 1:16

"Go therefore and make disciples of all the nations, baptizing them in the name of the Father and of the Son and of the Holy Spirit, teaching them to observe all things that I have commanded you; and lo, I am with you always, even to the end of the age."

MATTHEW 28:19–20

"I say to you, whoever confesses Me before men, him the Son of Man also will confess before the angels of God. But he who denies Me before men will be denied before the angels of God."

LUKE 12:8–9

"Behold, I stand at the door and knock. If anyone hears My voice and opens the door, I will come in to him and dine with him, and he with Me."

REVELATION 3:20

HELP THE POOR AND HOMELESS

What can you possibly do to help the poor and the homeless? What specific steps can you take in obedience to Jesus' command to do exactly that? You can pray for the poor and the homeless—and for the people serving them. You can support financially those Christian organizations that serve the poor and homeless, and you can support individuals involved in that effort. And you yourself can serve. Go to a local outreach center that provides medical care, worship opportunities, and meals for the poor and homeless. When you do any of these, you are doing God's work.

Above all things have fervent love for one another, for "love will cover a multitude of sins." Be hospitable to one another without grumbling. As each one has received a gift, minister it to one another, as good stewards of the manifold grace of God.

1 PETER 4:8–10

Let brotherly love continue. Do not forget to entertain strangers, for by so doing some have unwittingly entertained angels. Remember the prisoners as if chained with them—those who are mistreated—since you yourselves are in the body also.

HEBREWS 13:1–3

Defend the poor and fatherless;
    Do justice to the afflicted and needy.
    Deliver the poor and needy;
    Free them from the hand of the wicked.

PSALM 82:3–4

Whoever has this world's goods, and sees his brother in need, and shuts up his heart from him, how does the love of God abide in him? My little children, let us not love in word or in tongue, but in deed and in truth.

1 JOHN 3:17–18

TRUST HIM

Each of us becomes a Christian when we choose to trust that Jesus' death on the cross is sufficient for the forgiveness of our sin. That step is the first of a lifelong journey of choosing to trust God every step of the way for the rest of your life. You choose to trust Him to teach, guide, and protect you; to go before you and beside you each day; to grow your faith; to redeem life's losses and pain; and to use you to introduce others to Him. As you exercise your muscle of faith, your faith will indeed grow stronger.

Trust in the LORD, and do good;
Dwell in the land, and feed on His faithfulness.

PSALM 37:3

He who keeps Israel
Shall neither slumber nor sleep.
The LORD is your keeper;
The LORD is your shade at your right hand.
The sun shall not strike you by day,
Nor the moon by night.

PSALM 121:4–6

Though He slay me, yet will I trust Him.
Even so, I will defend my own ways before Him.
He also shall be my salvation.

JOB 13:15–16

Know that the LORD has set apart for Himself him
who is godly;
The LORD will hear when I call to Him.
Be angry, and do not sin.
Meditate within your heart on your bed, and be still.
Offer the sacrifices of righteousness,
And put your trust in the LORD.

PSALM 4:3–5

Preserve me, O God, for in You I put my trust.
O my soul, you have said to the LORD,
"You are my Lord,
My goodness is nothing apart from You."

PSALM 16:1–2

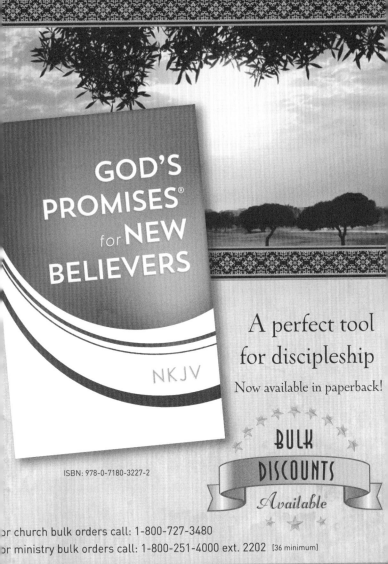

life. For God did not send His Son into t

-ld through Him might be saved. For G

-gotten Son, that whoever believes in Hi

-or God did not send His Son into the wor

-ugh Him might be saved. For God so lov

, that whoever believes in Him should r

-ot send His Son into the world to conden

-ght be saved. For God so loved the wor

-oever believes in Him should not peri

-d His Son into the world to condemn t

be saved. For God so loved the world th

-elieves in Him should not perish but ha

into the world to condemn the world, b

-or God so loved the world that He gave H

-im should not perish but have everlas

world to condemn the world, but that t

so loved the world that He gave His or

-hould not perish but have everlasting li

to condemn the world, but that the wor

-t send His Son into the world to conden

-ght be saved. For God did not send His S

Him should not perish but have everlas
orld to condemn the world, but that the
loved the world that He gave His only
ould not perish but have everlasting life
condemn the world, but that the world t
e world that He gave His only begotten
rish but have everlasting life. For God d
e world, but that the world through Him
at He gave His only begotten Son, that
t have everlasting life. For God did not
orld, but that the world through Him mi
e gave His only begotten Son, that whoev
erlasting life. For God did not send His
at the world through Him might be save
ly begotten Son, that whoever believes
g life. For God did not send His Son into
orld through Him might be saved. For G
gotten Son, that whoever believes in Hi
r God did not send His Son into the wo
rough Him might be saved. For God di
e world, but that the world through Him